The Virtual School Library

The Virtual School Library
Gateway to the Information Superhighway

Editor

Carol Collier Kuhlthau
Associate Professor
School of Communication, Information and Library Studies
Rutgers University

Associate Editors

M. Elspeth Goodin
and
Mary Jane McNally

1996
LIBRARIES UNLIMITED, INC.
Englewood, Colorado

NWST
AJN 8358

LIBRARIES UNLIMITED, INC.
P.O. Box 6633
Englewood, CO 80155-6633
1-800-237-6124

Project Editor: Tama J. Serfoss
Proofreader: Laura Taylor
Design and Layout: Robert D. Getchell

Library of Congress Cataloging-in-Publication Data

The virtual school library : gateway to the information superhighway /
  editor, Carol Collier Kuhlthau ; associate editors, M. Elspeth
Goodin and Mary Jane McNally.
    xiii, 161 p. 17x25 cm.
    Includes bibliographical references and index.
    ISBN 1-56308-336-1
    1. School libraries--United States--Data processing.   2. Digital
libraries--United States.   I. Kuhlthau, Carol Collier, 1937-   .
II. Goodin, M. Elspeth.   III. McNally, Mary Jane.
Z675.S3V835   1996
027.8'0285--dc20   95-52601
                                                                 CIP

Contents

Part II
Learning in the Electronic Information Age

Part III
Examples of Implementation

Part IV
Education for Library Media Specialists

Introduction

The nineties are bringing about important changes in school library media centers. The self-contained collection is giving way to a vast information network, frequently referred to as the virtual library, which is profoundly changing school library media programs. As computer technologies provide huge amounts of easily accessible information, attention turns beyond simply locating information to using information, and beyond library skills to information skills, which lead to information literacy and to the process of learning from information.

This book is a compilation of articles addressing the issue of the virtual school library. The authors present a wide range of perspectives on providing access to vast networks of information resources and enabling students to learn in an information-rich environment. While addressing many different aspects of the virtual library, the authors agree that the underlying concept of the "library without walls" shapes the library media program in important new ways.

During the publication of the 1994 edition of *School Library Media Annual*, the editors realized that while an entire section of SLMA was devoted to the topic of how "The Virtual Library Shapes the School Library Program," library media specialists needed and were demanding even more attention to the topic. This book pulls together the articles published in SLMA with additional pertinent pieces on practical applications for learning in the information-age school. Although this issue is in a continual state of change, the editors believe that this is an important addition to the literature.

The book is presented in four sections. The five articles in part I provide an overview of the virtual library, describe specific ways the technologies are being used, and give some recommendations for future development.

Virgil Blake lays the foundation for thinking about the impact of the virtual library on the school library media center in his bibliographic essay. He provides an extensive definition and explains the historical origins of the virtual library concept. The simplest definition is that the virtual library is a metaphor for the networked library. Stressing the importance of inclusion of the school library media program in the virtual library he asserts that, "school library media specialists are the only professionals in the position to demonstrate to all students the potential of the virtual library while attaining the goal of information literacy."

Jan Summers, library media specialist in Harrisburg, Missouri, reviews a wide range of resources available on the Internet and gives specific examples of how library media specialists and teachers are using these resources to enhance learning for elementary and secondary school students. She describes ways the Internet is being used to connect the school with the global community.

Michael Eisenberg and Peter Milbury discuss LM_NET, the library media specialists' electronic discussion group on the Internet. "The Internet" they say, "is the network of networks linking computer users throughout the world with each other and with a dazzling variety of resources." Library media specialists were among the first K-12 educators to see the potential of the network of global connectivity for their schools. This article describes the growth of LM_NET and reports on the importance of this type of information sharing.

Roxanne Mendrinos describes the application of CD-ROM technology, which has proved to be one of the most practical and efficient means for school library media centers to gain access to the virtual library. She offers examples of successful implementation in library media centers across the United States and a comprehensive overview of resources available through CD-ROM technology. She also details how to implement CD-ROM technology at the building and district level.

Dan Barron describes the current state of distance education, providing an update on his earlier writings. He asserts that, "the role of the school library media specialist in distance education, while greatly expanded in terms of knowledge required and activities to manage, remains basically the same—to help students and staff to become effective users of ideas and information." A comprehensive list of pertinent readings is included.

The three articles in part II address approaches to learning in the electronic environment. Providing technology and access is not enough to enhance learning; specific strategies and techniques are presented for guiding student learning in the information-age school.

Mark von Wodtke, author of *Minds over Media*, provides a stimulating discussion about ways to educate students to navigate the information highways. He stresses universal thinking skills, applying mental capacity in the use of new media. He shares some ways to teach important thinking skills for the electronic age.

Hilda Weisburg and Ruth Toor introduce 10 concepts that form the basis for a new information curriculum. "The information curriculum prepares students for selecting, interpreting, and using a flood of ideas, moving effortlessly between subject disciplines, and accessing sources from a variety of formats." They offer practical suggestions for implementation through end products, information sheets, and guided inquiry.

Carol Kuhlthau presents the process of learning from information as a key concept for the virtual school library. The information search process approach (ISPA) is described as a model for developing information skills that are fundamental to information literacy. Some basic abilities for using information that even the youngest children can learn are recommended along with strategies for implementing this approach.

The articles in part III present examples of implementation for school, district or county, and state level libraries.

Peter Milbury, one of the administrators of LM_NET listserv, explains how he got started in the world of the Internet at the building-level. In his letter to our readers, he describes his involvement with establishing access to resources on the Internet at Pleasant Valley High School in Chico, California, where he is the library media specialist.

Carol Kroll describes a highly successful countywide effort to implement information technologies into school library media programs. As Director of the Nassau School Library System in Nassau County, New York, she reports the progression of a long-range plan to change library media centers through the introduction of technology and curriculum planning. She relates how

through a long and deliberate process school library media specialists have not only changed their perceptions about their own role and the mission of the media center, but brought that vision to life in their school districts. Their accomplishments are giving schools state-of-the-art centers, which are changing the nature of classroom assignments and assessment, generating new relationships with other teachers and achieving respect from administrators and the school community at large.

Practical step-by-step procedures are offered.

Neah Lohr, consultant to the Wisconsin Department of Public Instruction, describes how one state is addressing the challenge of providing Internet access to PK-12 schools. Background and plans for the future are discussed in detail including some setbacks as well as successes.

In part IV, some new directions in education for library media specialists are recommended.

Kathleen Burnett and Mary Jane McNally consider changes in the education of library media specialists to prepare them for their role as leaders in information technology. They propose "an action agenda which will move the library media center from a locus of isolation to one of connection, from a print to a digital library." New course offerings are recommended for students pursuing school media certification, including one developed by Burnett for the M.L.S. program at Rutgers University.

Dianne Oberg, a faculty member at the University of Alberta in Canada, who was on a study leave to Australia, reports on her visit to four universities offering library education programs by distance education. Distance education is becoming an important consideration in library education in many places across the United States. This report from Australia is particularly timely as emerging technologies advance the capabilities to accommodate off-campus learning in the virtual classroom.

Kathleen Garland describes an in-service workshop on emerging technologies for library media specialists developed with a grant from the United States Department of Education through the Office of Library Programs. The goals of the workshop are to introduce library media specialists to the variety of information resources that may be accessed on the Internet and to provide them with experience in merging textual information from the Internet with visuals to create an educational product. Garland reports that, "We aim to empower participants to be building-level technology specialists in telecommunications who will teach other library media specialists, teachers, and students."

Taken together these articles by some of our leading thinkers and doers in the school library media field provide a comprehensive overview of the impact of information technology in school library media centers and offer some important recommendations for meeting the challenges of the virtual school library.

Contributors

Daniel D. Barron
Professor
College of Library and Information Science
University of South Carolina
Columbia, South Carolina

Virgil L. P. Blake
Associate Professor
Graduate School of Library and Informa-
 tion Studies
Queens College, CUNY
Flushing, New York

Kathleen Burnett
Assistant Professor
School of Communication, Information,
 and Library Studies
Rutgers University
New Brunswick, New Jersey

Michael B. Eisenberg
Professor, School of Information Studies
Director, ERIC Clearinghouse on Informa-
 tion and Technology
Syracuse University
Syracuse, New York

Kathleen Garland
Assistant Professor
School of Library and Information Science
University of Michigan
Ann Arbor, Michigan

Carol Kroll
Director, Nassau School Library System
Nassau Board of Cooperative Educational
 Services
Carle Place, New York

Carol Collier Kuhlthau
Associate Professor
School of Communication, Information
 and Library Studies
Rutgers University
New Brunswick, New Jersey

Neah J. Lohr
Consultant
Microcomputer and Instructional Technology
Wisconsin Department of Public Instruction
Madison, Wisconsin

Mary Jane McNally
Library Media Specialist
Ridge High School
Basking Ridge, New Jersey

Roxanne Baxter Mendrinos
Division Assistant
Instructional Services and Libraries
Foothill College
Los Altos Hills, California

Peter Milbury
Library Media Specialist
Pleasant Valley High School
Butte County, California

Dianne Oberg
Associate Professor
Department of Elementary Education
University of Alberta
Edmonton, Alberta, Canada

Jan Summers
Library Media Specialist
Harrisburg R-VIII School District
Harrisburg, Missouri

Ruth Toor
Library Media Specialist
Southern Boulevard School
Chatham, New Jersey

Mark von Wodtke
Professor
College of Environmental Design
California State Polytechnic University
Pomona, California

Hilda K. Weisburg
Library Media Specialist
Morristown High School
Morristown, New Jersey

Part I

Overview of Important Technologies Comprising the Virtual Library

1

The Virtual Library Impacts the School Library Media Center
A Bibliographic Essay

VIRGIL L. P. BLAKE

With the enactment of the Elementary and Secondary Education Act (ESEA) in 1965, the school library media center became a standard feature of public schools in the United States. This was a fortuitous time because the education establishment was under sustained attack by the critics of the text and test pedagogy of the time. These critics[1] advocated an indicative approach, which emphasized learning how to learn, and an individualized program. The corollary of this, as Francis Henne, Mary Gaver, and others were quick to point out, was the central role of the school library media center in providing the resources this mode of education required. Though the fervor of the critics and the acceptance of their agenda faded in the 1970s, the ideal of the school library media center as the center of the school's learning activities has remained constant.

Overlapping these developments was the evolution of a second hallmark of modern librarianship. After three years of deliberations, the new National Commission on Libraries and Information Science (NCLIS) published its report, *Toward a National Program for Library and Information Services: Goals for Action.*[2] This report called for the development of a national library network, which was defined as "an integrated system encompassing state networks, multi-state networks, and specialized networks in the public and private sector."[3] In 1978, the Task Force on the Role of the School Library Media Program in the National Program found that school library media centers held unique resources that would ensure their position as an equal partner in this proposed national library network, but that few were actually participating in existing networks. Over the course of the next decade, progress toward the proposed national library network was sporadic. Consequently, the place of the school library media center within this context was never established. In 1990, in the effort to obtain passage of the National Research and Education Network (NREN), the vision of a national library network reappeared in the guise of the "virtual library." In this paper the concept of the virtual library will be defined, the factors in its conception will be reviewed, the prerequisites for its success will be indicated, and, lastly, the implications of this concept for librarianship, with an emphasis on the school library media center, will be explored.

THE VIRTUAL LIBRARY

The term *virtual library* was first used by the Coalition for Networked Information (CNI), an organization of librarians, information specialists, and computer specialists. Its primary interest was the passage of the enabling legislation to create the NREN to electronically link scholars to information in all formats irrespective of its location. The simplest definition is that "the virtual library is a metaphor for the networked library."[4] Mitchell and Saunders make the concept clearer by indicating that the virtual library provides the user access not only to the local library's online public access catalog (OPAC) but to that of other libraries as well.[5] Weise broadens the concept by adding that the virtual library also affords its users access to "databases using the local library's online catalog or university or a network computer as a gateway."[6] Gapen refines the virtual library to

> the concept of remote access to the contents and services of libraries and other information resources, combining an onsite collection of current and heavily used materials in both print and electronic form, with an electronic network which provides access to, and delivery from, external world-wide library and commercial information and knowledge sources.[7]

Van Fleet and Wallace envision different levels of service from the virtual library. A minimalist approach "allows an individual to reach catalogs of libraries other than those of his or her own institution and possibly to directly place interlibrary loan requests."[8] A more sophisticated virtual library would permit the user to "be able to search other types of databases and retrieve complete texts of electronic publications."[9]

Butler describes the electronic collection plan developed by the Memex Research Institute as the basis for virtual libraries. There are four elements in this program: 1) public access information, 2) electronic image documents, 3) open network delivery, and 4) intellectual property management. Public access information refers to existing catalogs and published indexes in all formats (i.e., traditional print through CD-ROM as well as locally created access tools). Electronic image documents are electronically published materials in the collection that can be reproduced upon demand. Open network delivery is the ability to send information to a patron via a local area network (LAN) or other form of computer network. Intellectual property management is the use of software to monitor the use of materials to maintain privacy as well as comply with licensing agreements and copyright law. "By combining two or more E-Library collection operations under a common administrative set of policies," contends Butler, "individual libraries can form a virtual library."[10]

Based on the above, the virtual library has the following characteristics:

1. A local collection of materials that meet the information needs of the library's primary clientele

2. An OPAC, which identifies the holdings in that collection

3. The means to access abstracting and indexing services in machine readable form

4. Access to other databases to which the library subscribes

5. Telecommunications links to other libraries' OPACs and related information resources

6. Telecommunications links to other information agencies and their resources and services

7. The ability to send and receive information and data electronically

There are two prerequisites for the concept to become reality. First, the development of a computer network linked by wire or, preferably, fiber optic cables. A high-capacity, high-speed electronic communication system to permit scholars to share information and collaborate on projects is already in place. The virtual library only requires that libraries and information centers become directly involved in these research networks. A subsidiary problem lies in the area of protocols, which are the rules that govern the communication process between computers. One protocol common to all computers is ideal. As few protocols as possible is a more realistic goal. Second, the information and data to be shared among the constituent libraries in the virtual library must be easily transferable. This almost certainly dictates machine readable information. Traditional document delivery systems featuring physical movement of books or copies of journal articles, even with fax technology, may not be sufficient to ensure access in a timely fashion.

Despite the changes implicit in the acceptance of the virtual library concept, the mission of the library itself will be unchanged: "to facilitate access to documents."[11] This is no less binding on the school library media center.

WHY A VIRTUAL LIBRARY?

The virtual library concept appeals to the profession on a number of levels, not the least of which is economic. Over the last 12 years, the number of academic books published in North America alone has risen from 70,183 to 104,122, while the average price has increased from $21.98 to $49.53. Alexander's analysis[12] indicates that the number of serials in the Faxon database has grown from 38,000 titles in 1962 to 105,000 in 1988. At the same time, the average price of a serial rose 10.81 percent per year. However, he noted, there was a largely disproportionate increase in the number of scientific journals whose prices rose far faster than the norm. These developments were occurring at precisely the same time that the level of support for higher education was stabilizing, at best, or declining.

Caught up in the fate of the American economy, academic libraries, like public libraries and school library media centers, were less and less able to maintain existing collection levels. The search for alternatives, first examined by the National Enquiry for Scholarly Communication in 1979,[13] is now more determined because "the challenges confronting higher education are particularly severe and likely to be long lasting."[14] Downsizing will not be limited to corporate America. The financial crisis, however, is symptomatic of a much larger phenomenon, the breakdown of the scholarly communication process as we have known it.

Since Gutenburg, "knowledge has been communicated and stored largely through the use of printed documents."[15] Prior to World War II, the primary role of faculty in American colleges and universities was to teach.[16] Keeping current in one's discipline through reading was expected. Research and publication was not given special emphasis. In the post-World War II era, priorities for faculty have been transformed. Research and publication became the primary responsibility for faculty. The resulting pressure on faculty to publish was compounded by the tremendous expansion of higher education, especially since the 1960s. This combination was a prime factor in the great increase in the number of monographs and scholarly journals, which libraries, in turn, were expected to purchase. The cost of relying on the print media to sustain scholarly communication was the impetus for the National Enquiry for Scholarly Communication.

Collateral with the recognition of this problem, Apple, followed shortly by IBM, introduced the first personal computers (PCs). In the decade of the 1980s the PC advanced from handling family budgets to handling sophisticated multimedia programs. Now "all information is being transformed to digital form: books, movies, TV— everything."[17] Computer-based printing techniques made possible such online services as DIALOG and BRS. Full-text databases made their appearance with LEXIS and NEXIS. Video has been digitized since 1980 with the introduction of the 12-inch laserdisc. In 1993 the 5-inch CD videodisc was made available. Sound recordings were digitized in 1983 when the CD first appeared. Digital audio tape has also been developed. Over 2,500 electronic journals are now published.[18] Finally, the CD-ROM format for former print materials, both monographs and serials, is assuming an ever increasing role in the information environment.

It appears that the dominance of print is coming to an end. Ultimately, suggests Seiler, "information housed in books and other media will be stored in what [he calls] the digital electronic medium (DEM)."[19] Information in this form can be "created, captured, stored, manipulated, and communicated more usefully and less expensively than by other means."[20] As a result, contend Seiler and Surprenant, print, given its limitations in presenting motion, three-dimensional images, and sound, is being supplanted. "The information age," they conclude, "is not centered on the printed word; it is based on images, sounds and facts stored in databases."[21] In schools, Helsel predicts, "learning via printed symbols in textbooks will shift to learning via simulations. Curriculum materials will no longer be predominately text based but will be inquiry and symbol based."[22]

The logical extension of this is use of a sophisticated multimedia technique, virtual reality. Virtual reality is "a simulated experience . . . in a computer-generated three-dimensional multi-sensory real-time interactive environment."[23] The user, equipped with a head-mounted display unit, composed of a stereophonic headset and video goggles, and a data glove to maneuver objects in this created "space," interacts with the computer in a world in which he/she "can be immersed and is free to interact naturally with computer generated objects."[24] The introduction of these new technologies of information have the promise of adding to the classroom "information sources of the world and can foster flexible, creative and precise instruction that is targeted to the individual."[25] The school library media specialist, it follows, has the responsibility "to provide students and teachers with access to information and resources beyond what is tritely called 'traditional.' "[26] This implies that the school library media specialist has a vested interest in the virtual library concept.

LIBRARIES AND INFORMATION TECHNOLOGY

Beginning with the development of the MARC II format for cataloging records in the mid-1960s, libraries have continuously adapted computer-based information technology. The MARC II format led directly to the creation of bibliographic utilities such as OCLC, the Research Libraries Information Network (RLIN), and the Western Library Network (WLN) for the purpose of storing and supplying cataloging data to member libraries. Throughout the 1970s, libraries added computerized circulation systems, interlibrary loan systems, acquisitions systems, and serials control systems. These were stand-alone turn-key systems developed by libraries themselves or vendors.[27] The culmination of this process was the introduction of the online public access catalog (OPAC) in 1980.

Adapting the computer for library operations was not limited to technical services. In the 1970s, online databases (essentially machine readable abstracting and indexing services) offered by independent vendors such as DIALOG Information Services (DIALOG) or Bibliographic Retrieval Systems (BRS), became elements of the library's repertoire. By the end of the 1970s, both technical service librarians and reference librarians were expected to have basic competencies with these technologies.

The 1980s saw further refinements of computer-based technologies in both areas of specialization in librarianship. The independent stand-alone turn-key systems added authority control features. Integrated systems were developed by vendors to use cataloging copy, from whatever source, as the basis for all other technical services functions—acquisitions, authority work, circulation, serials control, interlibrary loans, and OPACS. The role of online databases in reference work also changed. Many libraries now subscribe to the CD-ROM versions of databases previously accessible through vendors such as DIALOG. The newer CD-ROM versions were made directly available to the public because connect time charges were a greatly diminished factor. As libraries entered the 1990s, they were "adding table[s] of contents to OPACs, providing abstracts, and moving toward full text retrieval."[28]

Libraries, it would seem, have considerable experience in adapting computer-based technologies. The virtual library concept presumes skills in this area. But it must be noted that the last two decades have focused on the individual library, its internal operations, and information services for its own public. The virtual library concept calls for the provision of access to information resources beyond the library itself. With everything that is already in place as a base, all that is required is the means to this access—a network.

LIBRARIES AND NETWORKS

Networking, as originally used by librarians, encompassed a broad range of cooperative activities usually featuring resource sharing. By the mid-1970s networking had been refined to mean cooperative activities involving computers and telecommunications.[29] In that era, this referred to terminals in a library connected to a remote mainframe computer. The terminals themselves served only as conduits the mainframe, which held the data and performed tasks requested of it through the terminals. Both OCLC and RLIN are good examples of this type of network.

In the 1980s, microcomputers became increasingly more powerful, cheaper, and ubiquitous. This evolving technology made possible the research network in which "PCs and mainframes can all intercommunicate."[30] Within this setting any microcomputer can "process data, or ask any other computer to process data for them; no matter what their size they are all equals in the network."[31] Individual scholars could directly communicate with each other over this type of network. These networks, called peer-to-peer networks, can vary in size from campuswide local area networks (LANs) to national networks. Libraries, if they are to provide such access to external resources as the virtual library concept requires, must be involved with this type of state, regional, and national computer network.

At the present time there are two well-known national networks, BITNET and Internet. BITNET is "used primarily for the interchange of files and electronic mail."[32] It is a cooperative venture of colleges and universities that agree to use mainframe computers in their academic computer centers and phone lines for communicating. The Internet, however, "supports mail, file transfer, remote log on and other types of direct real time computer-to-computer interaction."[33] These additional services are needed to operationalize the virtual library concept.

The Internet can trace its roots to the Defense Advanced Projects Agency's ARPANET, a computer network "limited to organizations involved in government sponsored research in networking and computer science."[34] Its immediate parent is the National Science Foundation's NSFNET, a computer network of six supercomputer centers, mid-level networks, and local (i.e., campus-level) networks. NSFNET is a member of the Internet, which is really "a group of interconnected national, regional and campus networks that use the same communications protocols."[35] At the pinnacle of the three-tiered hierarchy that is the Internet are national computer networks like NSFNET, the Department of Defense's MILNET, and the Department of Energy's HepNET. At the second level are the mid-level networks such as NYSERNET, the Merit Computer Network, and THEnet (Texas High Education Network). At the third level are countless local computer networks composed of individual library catalogs and specialized databases such as Dartmouth College's Dante Project. Through the Internet, "users can exchange electronic mail messages with colleagues across the United States and in foreign countries . . . subscribe to bulletin boards through which participants exchange views and information on a variety of topics . . . [and] access library catalogs. . . ."[36]

The Internet has become a highly congested information highway. Its popularity was complicated by its limitations "in the amount of data . . . [the users] can transmit by speed (the rate at which data moves across the network) and bandwidth (the volume of data that can be transmitted at one time)."[37] These limitations were a factor in the introduction of the National High Performance Computer Technology Act by then-Senator Gore in 1989. A major element of this proposed legislation was the National Research and Education Network (NREN), which, it was hoped, would resolve the speed and bandwidth problems.

In the spring of 1990, the Coalition for Networked Information was formed to lobby for passage of the act. The NREN was envisioned as "a partnership of government, education, and industry"[38] that would create a comprehensive national computer network. Supporters argued that the NREN was "essential for the United States to maintain its competitive edge in the world."[39] The NREN, it was stated, would not be limited to electronic mail and access to scientific research. Its mission was "to include access to information resources such as library information systems, databases, information services, and electronic publishing."[40] The NREN was precisely what the virtual library required. It was approved by Congress and signed by President Bush in 1991. Though many of the operational details were largely unresolved, the technological support system the virtual library concept requires will be put into place in the course of the next few years.

ISSUES AND CONCERNS

With the virtual library concept as the lodestone for a national information network, and the new information environment implicit in the digitization process outlined by Seiler, a vision of the library of the later twenty-first century has been proposed. Several issues, however, will need to be addressed as librarianship gropes its way toward the future. The first of these involves the question of inclusion and exclusion. The virtual library and its mandatory prerequisite, a national computer network, have, to date, been the province of the academic library. All the computer networks that are or will be part of the projected national information complex (BITNET, Internet, and NREN) are affiliated with academic research facilities. Neither the public library nor the school library media center have been factors in developments thus far. It would follow that the prime beneficiaries of the virtual library will be faculty and students affiliated with a college or university serving as a node for the network. This somewhat elitist vision excludes unaffiliated scholars, the general public, and students in both public and private schools.

This exclusion makes little sense if the library as an institution is to be a key element in the information age. Excluding the public library and school library media center guarantees that the "virtual library will be inaccessible to a large segment of the user community."[41] This concern is magnified if Seiler is correct and the digital electronic medium (DEM) supplants traditional print and nonprint information sources. The chances of creating an information underclass to accompany America's seemingly permanent economic underclass are greatly increased. Because a major argument in support of the NREN was its role in maintaining America's competitive edge, ignoring the information needs of the public is extremely shortsighted.

This is compounded in the case of the school library media center. Since the inception of ESEA, one could be certain that all students in public schools had direct access to a library. Over the course of the school year, a major role of the school library media specialist, particularly at the elementary level, is to provide bibliographic instruction to ensure that students can identify appropriate information resources, locate them, and use them to complete various educational assignments. In short, a primary responsibility of the school library media specialist is to develop information-literate students. The role of the school library media specialist, in this regard, has always been critical. Effective school library media programs, with the advantage of a captive audience, are primary means for inculcating students with the ability to use libraries and information centers to resolve problems in their future educational endeavors and in their lives.

To fully prepare today's students to effectively use the full range of information resources that will be available to them, the school library media center, it would seem, ought to be included in the emerging virtual library. It makes little sense to exclude students until and unless they become affiliated with a college or university and then hope they will survive in this richer environment.

Both public librarians and school library media specialists then have a vital interest in the virtual library concept because it is serving as the goal in the development of the national information complex. In both settings, exclusion will diminish the chances of fulfilling the information needs of their respective publics. "If the library is perceived as being irrelevant," caution Van Fleet and Wallace, "it will lose support."[42] Ironically, the onset of the information age could usher in the decline, if not the demise, of the library. Seiler and Surprenant have speculated that the establishment of the electronic library, fully equipped with DEM and full-text databases and accessible at all times by remote users, might result in far fewer libraries.[43] These libraries, due to the expenses of operating such enterprises, might be state controlled. The plausibility of scenarios such as this should serve as a wake-up call. School library media specialists must become directly involved in delineating the structure and governing the national information complex that the virtual library idea represents.

Given the necessity of including the school library media center within the virtual library concept, a second major issue is the financial support of this structure. Both the BITNET and the Internet are supported by member institutions and federal funds. The NREN, as currently conceived, does not provide federal funding for the operation of the network. Federal monies appropriated for the NREN are to be used for research and development. The cost of inclusion is not inconsiderable. Participants in the virtual library will have to "budget for computer hardware and new releases of software."[44] In addition, the library or information center will have to decide which resources it should "purchase and retain on site, and [to which it] should purchase access."[45] Finally, the library will have to factor in the "cost of increased interlibrary loan and document delivery."[46]

Lago reports that the American Library Association's Washington Office has estimated that "$75.25 million would provide each [public] library with a $2,000 personal computer with a 9600 baud modem and communications software ($30 million) and cover the first year dial up to the local point of presence ($37.5 million), a $56,000 average first year salary and benefits for a computer/telecommunications consultant at each state library agency ($3.25 million) and $300 for training at each library ($4.5 million)."[47] This estimate, adds Lago, does not include connect time charges or the phone bill. A possible source of this financial support might be the Library Services and Construction Act (LSCA). No similar estimate for school library media centers has been calculated, but, given their far greater numbers, they would require much more than the $75.25 million projected for public libraries. This estimation must be done to realistically plan for inclusion of the school library media center in the envisioned virtual library configuration. One possible vehicle for this might be legislation modeled on the original ESEA.

Progress toward the realization of any national information complex along the lines of the virtual library "will require considerable planning and coordination at the national level."[48] In the virtual library context, each library or information center will have to clearly detail its "mission, goals, objectives and service roles."[49] The two primary foci are personnel and the collection itself. The siren song of the virtual library, warns Shaughnessy, is that "it may relieve libraries, in the minds of campus decision makers, of the responsibility to build local collections."[50] Overreliance on the principle of access to remote collections and other resources may lead to asking "why the library should buy any print material at all."[51] Individual libraries should not take advantage of their peers by cutting back on collection development activities due to fiscal or other local pressures just because other libraries or resources are readily accessible in the virtual library setting. There is still a basic responsibility to meet the majority of the information needs of the library's typical clientele. "Network strength cannot serve as a substitute for local collection strength," warn Van Fleet and Wallace, "nor as a cure for institutional weakness."[52]

This responsibility to maintain strong local collections will be more complex in the virtual library environment. Acquisitions budgets will have to be sufficient to maintain needed current print materials and, simultaneously, incorporate new electronic media. This will be the case until the transition to Seiler's DEM is complete (or as complete as it can be). In the electronically based information environment associated with the virtual library, contend Smith and Johnson, "large collections will no longer be essential."[53] Libraries, it follows, will need to "acquire only the most heavily and regularly used material for processing and retention."[54] Given the results of weeding studies,[55] this is not only possible but potentially a source of savings that could be used to participate in the national information complex implicit in the virtual library concept.

A second source of funding lies in the increased use of interlibrary loan and document delivery services. Shaughnessy argues that this facet of the virtual library may be illusionary because "many of our libraries are already finding it impossible to keep up with existing levels of interlibrary loan traffic."[56] The mitigating factor here is the growth in recent years in the number of machine readable products, especially in the CD-ROM format. As a result, "methods of rapid information transfer have improved enormously."[57] If this progress continues, libraries will be able to rely, with some confidence, on the principle of access to remote collections and information services. The pressure for large comprehensive collections will be greatly reduced.

The ideal of developing more focused local collections supplemented by access to other collections has been a feature in library literature since the 1970s.[58] Like all of its predecessors, the success of the virtual library rests upon the "long unfulfilled prospect of meaningful research library cooperative collection development."[59] The necessity for planning and maintaining strong local library collections is equally important for public library and school library media center participation in the virtual library as it is envisioned. Unfortunately, the school library media specialists may be in the same situation they found themselves in 15 years ago. "Current professional literature," Barron reported, suggests they (school library media specialists) were not included at the outset, are not presently included with specifically designated responsibilities, and have no designated role in future projects."[60] This status is not professionally tenable and should not be tolerated by school library media specialists.

The digitization of information, a key ingredient in the virtual library concept, brings with it some other unique problems. Throughout the print era, the materials included in library collections had some imprimatur of quality. Books had to be selected for publication and even then were carefully edited and reviewed. Journals, especially scholarly journals, published articles that had survived the refereeing process. Sound recordings, films, video, and other nonprint formats all were made available after analogous selection processes. As electronic publishing, in the form of Kurzweil's virtual book[61] and electronic serials, assumes a larger role in scholarly communication, many of these filters will disappear and, with them, the *presumption* of quality. The nature of the relationship between libraries and publishers will change, suggest Seiler and Surprenant, because there will no longer be a reason for multiple copies of items. Equally important is the need to ensure that early editions of works survive.[62] In the print era this was not a problem. In an electronic setting, older information can easily be replaced by newer while erasing the pre-existing data. Seiler and Surprenant also point out the ease with which information could be destroyed by a computer virus or altered by a "hacker."

By far the most heated arguments generated by the digitization of information center on intellectual property and copyright. "The ease with which digital information can be copied from one medium to another raises significant concerns for the ownership of intellectual property."[63] Technological improvements to ensure the timely exchange of information will foster a "heated debate about who should control the intellectual property rights involved."[64] For school library media centers, the use of materials protected by copyright in instruction has been a sensitive issue. Once again, school library media specialists have a vested interest in the resolution of this issue. There is a proposed solution in the form of the SHARer auditing software system. SHARer would be responsible for the "management of data input, transaction recording, control management and licensor or royalty fee payment."[65] The credibility of the virtual library, for all its constituents, requires an effective response to this and the other unique problems associated with the rise of electronic formats.

There remains one other aspect of the virtual library concept that must be considered. An underlying assumption of the virtual library's remote access to other libraries' catalogs and databases is that the means to deliver the information found in other libraries' collections in a timely fashion are available. But what other libraries and other information agencies will be making available has not been carefully detailed. Having access to a wide range of other libraries' OPACs may not be a significant improvement over access to OCLC's Online Union Catalog with its location codes. There may be more value in having access to locally created information resources, but this will be the case only if the institution chooses to make these resources available to other libraries and information centers. The library's obligations in this regard remain unclear. It would seem that a major aspect of the planning for the virtual library would require that designated libraries and other information centers be given primary responsibilities in specific areas. This is one of the purposes of the Conspectus approach to collection evaluation.

In the process of clarifying responsibilities, it would seem that school library media centers have a unique role that derives from their obligation to support the curriculum. This mission could easily generate a locally created resource that would be of interest to other libraries. If the New York City Board of Education's Office of Multicultural Education, for example, were to develop a unique information source in the teaching of multiculturalism in the elementary school, it would be appropriate to make this available through the network that is the virtual library. The potential audience for such a resource could include colleges and universities with programs in education as well as other school library media centers. Including school library media centers in the virtual library setting and assigning them primary responsibility for resources of this sort would ensure that unique local resources were made accessible. Presently, there is no guarantee that this would be the case.

THE VIRTUAL LIBRARIAN

Seiler and Surprenant suggest that the electronic library will require "specialists in collection development, database maintenance, information input, and searching." There is the possibility that these electronic libraries will be administered by "those with extensive hardware and software backqrounds." This might result, they warn, in the loss of a professional ethic that has "resisted censorship and championed retaining all ideas, not only popular ones."[66] Though this somewhat apocalyptic scenario is speculative, it must be recognized that the concept of the virtual library carries with it changes in staffing and professional responsibilities within libraries and information centers.

At the very least, "library staff will need new and more sophisticated skills as they work with emerging technologies. Computer networking skills will be base requirements."[67] It is the task of schools of library and information science, through mandated courses in information technology for all students, to ensure that new professionals "have additional computing skills in telecommunications . . . [and] broad skills with a wide range of online systems."[68] The virtual library concept assumes that librarians will have access to hundreds of OPACs and a number of online databases. Public service librarians, especially reference librarians, will have "to know, at least in passing, the protocols for every link."[69] An added responsibility will be knowing how to search in all the catalogs and databases to which the library has access. Reference librarians will be expected to "identify and evaluate electronic information sources for purchase,"[70] as they have traditionally done with print resources.

Reference service itself may change. Reference librarians might discover that it is easier to respond to ready reference questions by immediately accessing the computer than it is to "investigate several tools in the stacks."[71] Responses to higher-order reference questions will almost certainly require sophisticated knowledge of other library collections or databases. This will require a different emphasis or mode of instruction in reference and database-searching courses for library and information science educators. Navigating through other library catalogs and databases also has implications for courses in technical services and library automation.

"Training naive users to become competent in accessing and understanding various types of electronic sources" is yet another responsibility for public service and reference librarians in the virtual library context.[72] Conceivably, they will be given the task of providing instruction to other librarians and other staff members as well as to the users. This task may carry with it the ability to "contribute to the production of library instructional materials for the use of these products."[73] It will be necessary to have "effective menus and help screens to capture the bulk of user expectations."[74]

School library media specialists who are expected to be familiar with instruction technology as well as librarianship may have an advantage in designing effective bibliographic instruction programs to meet these ends. This is another way school library media specialists can make a significant contribution to the success of the virtual library concept and its ability to serve students and the public at large.

Alterations in professional responsibilities will not be limited to public service and reference librarians. As digitally based information resources assume a larger proportion of the library or information center's repertoire, traditional methods of organizing information for retrieval will be scrutinized. Technical services librarians should begin to develop "more powerful indexing systems to help . . . sort, control and manipulate the information."[75] Cutter's lamented golden age might have merely set the stage for a renewed quest for the more powerful searching techniques required in a digitally based information environment.

THE VIRTUAL SCHOOL LIBRARY MEDIA CENTER?

Van Fleet and Wallace feel that the public library and school library media center are "unlikely to have meaningful access to electronic networks."[76] Acceptance of this will ensure that the "virtual library will be virtually inaccessible to a large segment of the library user community."[77] This is unacceptable if the goal of the virtual library is to provide the means to remain economically competitive.

School library media centers have the basic prerequisities for participation in the virtual library concept. Surveys by Miller and Shontz indicate that, by 1989, 42 percent of school library media centers had OPACs.[78] With the increasing availability of MARC II cataloging records through vendors (Marcive, DIALOG, and WILSONLINE, for example) and the ongoing development of integrated systems, this number will continue to grow. CD-ROM technology, report Eisenberg and Spitzer, is placing machine readable abstracting and indexing services and full-text databases within the reach of school library media centers.[79] Supplementing these minimal requirements are other factors that must be emphasized. School library media centers, dealing primarily with children and young adults, are a likely source for unique resources that would be of interest to both public libraries and colleges and universities with schools of education. Finally, it must not be forgotten that school library media specialists are the only professionals in the position to demonstrate to all students the potential of the virtual library while attaining the goal of information literacy. Recalling the fate of the Task Force on the Role of the School Library Media Program in the National Program, it becomes apparent that school library media specialists must prepare themselves and ensure their inclusion in the virtual library—for the sake of their profession and their students.

NOTES

1.   James Herndon, *The Way It's Spozed to Be* (New York: Simon and Schuster, 1968); John Holt, *How Children Fail* (New York: Delta Books, 1964); Ivan Illich, *Deschooling Society* (New York: Harrow, 1971); Herb Kohl, *36 Children* (New York: New American Library, 1967); Jonathan Kozol, *Death at an Early Age* (Boston: Houghton Mifflin, 1967); Charles Silberman, *Crisis in the Classroom: Remaking of American Education* (New York: Random House, 1970); Neil Postman and Charles Weingartner, *Teaching as a Subversive Activity* (New York: Delacorte, 1969).

2.   National Commission on Libraries and Information Science, *Toward a National Program for Library and Information Services: Goals for Action* (Washington, DC: National Commission on Libraries and Information Science, 1975).

3.   Ibid., 49.

4. LaVerna Saunders, "The Virtual Library: Computers in Libraries Canada," *Computers in Libraries* 12, no. 11 (December 1992): 72.

5. Maurice Mitchell and LaVerna M. Saunders, "The Virtual Library: An Agenda for the 1990s," *Computers in Libraries* 11, no. 4 (April 1991): 811.

6. Frieda O. Weise, "Developments in Health Sciences Libraries Since 1974: From Physical Entity to the Virtual Library," *Library Trends* 42, no. 1 (summer 1993): 6.

7. D. Kaye Gapen, "The Virtual Library: Knowledge Society and the Librarian," in *The Virtual Library: Visions and Realities*, ed. LaVerna M. Saunders (Westport, CT: Meckler, 1992), 1.

8. Connie Van Fleet and Danny P. Wallace, "Virtual Virtue," *RQ* 32, no. 3 (spring 1993): 306.

9. Ibid.

10. Brett Butler, "The Electronic Library Program: Developing Networked Electronic Library Collections," *Library Hi Tech* 9, no. 2 (1991): 23.

11. W. David Penniman, "The Library of Tomorrow: A Universal Window Serving Independent Problem Solvers," *Library Hi Tech* 10, no. 4 (1992): 24.

12. Adrian Alexander, "Serial Pricing in the International Market: Fifteen Years of Faxon Experience," *Library Administration & Management* 4, no. 1 (winter 1989): 27-32.

13. *Scholarly Communication: The Report of the National Enquiry* (Baltimore, MD: Johns Hopkins Press, 1979).

14. Eldred Smith and Peggy Johnson, "How to Survive the Present While Preparing for the Future: A Research Library Strategy," *College & Research Libraries* 54, no. 5 (September 1993): 389.

15. David W. Lewis, "Inventing the Electronic University," *College & Research Libraries* 49, no. 4 (July 1988): 291.

16. C. B. Osborn, *Academic Research and Library Resources: Changing Patterns in America* (Westport, CT: Greenwood Press, 1979).

17. Lauren Seiler and Thomas Surprenant, "When We Get the Libraries We Want Will We Want the Libraries We Get?" *Wilson Library Bulletin* 65, no. 10 (June 1991): 29.

18. *Ulrich's International Periodical Directory: A Classified Guide to Current Periodicals Foreign and Domestic* (New York: Bowker, 1932-).

19. Lauren H. Seiler, "The Concept of Book in the Age of the Digital Electronic Medium," *Library Software Review* 11, no. 1 (January-February 1992): 20.

20. Lauren Seiler and Thomas Surprenant, "When We Get the Libraries," 29.

21. Ibid.

22. Sandra Helsel, "Virtual Reality and Education," *Educational Technology* 32, no. 5 (May 1992): 41.

23. Gary Ferrington and Kenneth Loge, "Virtual Reality: A New Learning Environment," *The Computing Teacher* 19, no. 7 (April 1992): 16.

24. R. J. Stone, "Virtual Reality and Cyperspace: From Science Fiction to Science Fact," *Information Services & Use* 11 (1991): 284.

25. Michael B. Eisenberg and Kathleen L. Spitzer, "Information Technology and Services in Schools," in *Annual Review of Information Science and Technology 1991*, vol. 26, ed. Martha E. Williams (Medford, NJ: Learned Information, 1991), 244.

26. Daniel D. Barron, "Distance Education and School Library Media Specialists," in *School Library Media Annual, 1991*, vol. 9, ed. Jane Bundy Smith and J. Gordon Coleman (Englewood, CO: Libraries Unlimited, 1991), 24.

27. James Rice, *Introduction to Library Automation* (Littleton, CO: Libraries Unlimited, 1984); Dennis Reynolds, *Library Automation: Issues and Applications* (New York: Bowker, 1985); William Saffady, *Introduction to Library Automation for Librarians* (Chicago: American Library Association, 1989).

28. Sue Levy, "Perspectives on Networking," *Computers in Libraries* 12, no. 5 (May 1992): 63.

29. Barbara Markuson, "Library Networks: Progress and Problems," in *The Information Age*, ed. Donald P. Hammer (Metuchen, NJ: Scarecrow Press, 1975); Brett Butler, "State of the Nation in Networking," *Journal of Library Automation* 8, no. 3 (September 1975): 200-220.

30. Gary Cleveland, "Canadian Libraries and the Emerging Information Network," *Canadian Library Journal* 49, no. 5 (October 1992): 369.

31. Ibid.

32. Clifford A. Lynch, "The Growth of Computer Networks: A Status Report," *Bulletin of the American Society for Information Science* 16, no. 5 (June/July 1990): 10.

33. Ibid.

34. Caroline R. Arms, "A New Information Infrastructure," *Online* 14, no. 5 (September 1990): 17.

35. Ibid.

36. Roberta A. Corbin, "The Development of the National Research and Education Network," *Information Technology and Libraries* 10, no. 3 (September 1991): 215.

37. Ibid.

38. Barbara L. Scheid, "Overview of NREN and CNI: How They Impact Your Library, Presented by Jane Ryland," *Information Technology and Libraries* 11, no. 1 (March 1992): 43.

39. Roberta Corbin, "National Research and Education Network," 215.

40. Clifford A. Lynch, "Computer Networks," 11.

41. Connie Van Fleet and Danny P. Wallace, "Virtual Virtue," 307.

42. Ibid., 308.

43. Lauren Seiler and Thomas Surprenant, "The Virtual Information Center: Scholars and Information in the Twenty-First Century," in *Libraries and the Future*, ed. F. W. Lancaster (New York: Haworth Press, 1993): 157-80.

44. LaVerna M. Saunders, "The Virtual Library Today," *Library Administration & Management* 6, no. 2 (spring 1992): 68.

45. Ibid.

46. Ibid.

47. Karen Nadder Lago, "The Internet and the Public Library: Practical and Political Realities," *Computers in Libraries* 13, no. 9 (October 1993): 67.

48. Eldred Smith and Peggy Johnson, "Survive the Present," 395.

49. LaVerna Saunders, "The Virtual Library," 72.

50. Thomas W. Shaughnessy "The Real Costs and Financial Challenges of Library Networking: Part 2," in *Networks, Open Access and Virtual Libraries: Implications for the Research Library*, ed. Brett Sutton and Charles H. Davis (Urbana, IL: University of Illinois at Urbana-Champaign, Graduate School of Library and Information Science, 1991), 124.

51. Ibid.

52. Connie Van Fleet and Danny P. Wallace, "Virtual Virtue," 308.

53. Eldred Smith and Peggy Johnson, "Survive the Present," 391.

54. Ibid., 392.

55. Allen Kent and others, *The Use of Library Materials: The University of Pittsburgh Study* (New York: Dekker, 1979); Stanley J. Slote, *Weeding Library Collections* (Englewood, CO: Libraries Unlimited, 1989); Richard W. Trueswell, "User Circulation Satisfaction vs. Size of Holdings at Three Academic Libraries," *College & Research Libraries* 30, no. 3 (May 1969): 204-13.

56. Thomas W. Shaughnessy, "Real Costs," 125.

57. Eldred Smith and Peggy Johnson, "Virtual Virtue," 393.

58. Mary Duncan Carter, Wallace John Bonk, and Rose Mary Magrill, *Building Library Collections*, 4th edition (Metuchen, NJ: Scarecrow Press, 1974).

59. Eldred Smith and Peggy Johnson, "Survive the Present," 395.

60. Daniel D. Barron, "Distance Education," 23.

61. Raymond Kurzweil, "The Virtual Library," *Library Journal* 118, no. 5 (March 1993): 54-55.

62. Lauren Seiler and Thomas Surprenant, "The Virtual Information Center," 157-80.

63. David W. Lewis, "Electronic University," 297.

64. Brett Butler, "Electronic Editions of Serials: The Virtual Library Model," *Serials Review* 18, no. 1/2 (spring/summer 1992): 105.

65. Brett Butler, "The Electronic Library Program: Developing Networked Electronic Library Collections," *Library Hi Tech* 9, no. 2 (1991): 25.

66. Lauren Seiler and Thomas Surprenant, "When We Get the Libraries," 31.

67. LaVerna Saunders, "The Virtual Library," 72.

68. Maurice Mitchell and LaVerna M. Saunders, "Virtual Library," 10.

69. Connie Van Fleet and Danny P. Wallace, "Virtual Virtue," 308.

70. LaVerna M. Saunders, "The Virtual Library Revisited," *Computers in Libraries* 12, no. 10 (November 1992): 54.

71. Ibid., 53.

72. Maurice Mitchell and LaVerna M. Saunders, "Virtual Library," 8.

73. LaVerna M. Saunders, "The Virtual Library Revisited," 54.

74. Linda Joyce Kosmin, "Electronic Reference Desk: Prospects, Promises, Realities," in *National Online Meeting Proceedings-1990*, ed. Martha E. Williams (Medford, NJ: Learned Information, 1990), 218.

75. Maurice Mitchell and LaVerna M. Saunders, "Virtual Library," 10.

76. Connie Van Fleet and Danny P. Wallace, "Virtual Virtue," 307.

77. Ibid.

78. Marilyn L. Miller and Marilyn L. Shontz, "Expenditures for Resources in School Library Media Centers, FY '88-'89," *School Library Journal* 35, no. 10 (June 1989): 31-40.

79. Michael B. Eisenberg and Kathleen L. Spitzer, "Information Technology," 258.

BIBLIOGRAPHY

Allen, Brockenbrough, S. "Virtualities." In *Educational Media and Technology Yearbook, 1991*, vol. 17, edited by Brenda Banyan-Broadbent and R. Kent Wood. Englewood, CO: Libraries Unlimited, 1991, 47-53.

Bailey, Charles W., Jr. "Intelligent Multimedia Computer Systems: Emerging Information Resources in the Network Environment." *Library Hi Tech* 8, no. 1 (1990): 29-41.

Bell, Gordon. "Steps Toward a National Research Telecommunications Network." *Library Hi Tech* 6, no. 1 (1988): 33-36.

Boucher, Rick. "The Vision of the National High-Performance Computing Act of 1991." *Information Technology and Libraries* 11, no. 1 (March 1992): 56-58.

The Bowker Annual Library and Book Trade Almanac. New Providence, NJ: Bowker, 1993.

Brownrigg, Edwin B. "The Internet as an External Economy: The Emergence of the Invisible Hand." *Library Administration Management* 5, no. 2 (spring 1991): 95-97.

Dede, Christopher J. "The Future of Multimedia: Bridging to Virtual Worlds." *Educational Technology* 32, no. 5 (May 1992): 54-60.

Drummond, Louis. "Going Beyond Online." *Online* 14, no. 5 (September 1990): 6-8.

LaRue, James. "The Library Tomorrow: A Virtual Certainty." *Computers in Libraries* 13, no. 2 (February 1993): 14-16.

_____. "The Virtual Library." *Wilson Library Bulletin* 65, no. 7 (March 1991): 100-102.

Martin, Susan K. "Defining 'It': NREN's Opportunities for Librarians." In *Networks, Open Access and Virtual Libraries: Implications for the Research Library,* edited by Brett Sutton and Charles Davis. Urbana, IL: University of Illinois at Urbana-Champaign Graduate School of Library and Information Science, 1991, 61-73.

Miller, Carmen. "*Online* Interviews Dr. Thomas A. Furness III Virtual Reality Pioneer." *Online* 16, no. 6 (November 1992): 14-27.

_____. "Virtual Reality and Online Databases: Will 'Look and Feel' Literally Mean 'Look' and 'Feel'?" *Online* 16, no. 6 (November 1992): 12-13.

Nugent, William. "Virtual Reality: Advanced Imaging Special Effects Let You Roam in Cyberspace." *Journal of the American Society for Information Science* 42, no. 8 (September 1991): 609-17.

Osborn, C. B. *Academic Research and Library Resources: Changing Patterns in America.* Westport, CT: Greenwood Press, 1979.

Poultner, Alan. "Towards a Virtual Reality Library." *Aslib Proceedings* 45, no. 1 (January 1993): 11-17.

Raitt, David. "The Electronic Library Manager's Guide to Virtual Reality." *The Electronic Library* 9, no. 1 (February 1991): 3-5.

Romkey, John. "Whither Cyberspace?" *Journal of the American Society for Information Science* 42, no. 8 (September 1991): 618-20.

Seiler, Lauren, and Thomas Surprenant. "The Virtual Information Center: Scholars and Information in the Twenty-First Century." In *Libraries and the Future,* edited by F. Wilfred Lancaster. New York: Haworth Press, 1993, 157-80.

Swisher, Robert, Kathleen L. Spitzer, Barbara Spriestersbach, Tim Markus, and Jerry M. Burris. "Telecommunications for School Library Media Centers." *School Library Media Quarterly* 19 (spring 1991): 153-60.

Task Force on the Role of the School Library Media Program in the National Program. *The Role of the School Library Media Program in Networking.* Washington, DC: National Commission on Libraries and Information Science, 1978.

"The Virtual Library." *Computers in Libraries* 12, no. 6 (June 1992): 26.

2

Using the Internet to Enhance Teaching and Learning

JAN SUMMERS

A third grade teacher helps her students correspond with students in Zimbabwe to learn about their culture. A media specialist determines the current status of endangered species legislation in Congress for a biology teacher. A German teacher obtains information from NASA about the space shuttle flight on which German scientists are conducting experiments. A high school student locates census information for a report. A guidance counselor provides a student with scholarship information from a state university.

What all of the above situations have in common is that they involve the use of telecommunications. Access to the Internet allows users to communicate with people throughout the world using electronic mail; subscribe to lists through which persons with common interests share ideas, ask questions, and disseminate information; and search through hundreds of different networks for specific information.

WHAT IS THE INTERNET?

What exactly is the Internet? In his book *The Whole Internet User's Guide and Catalog*, Ed Krol defines the Internet as "the world-wide 'network of networks' that are connected to each other" (1992, 358). The Internet encompasses all sizes of networks, from local area networks (LANs) to regional networks to the NSFnet (called the "backbone" of the United States-based part of the Internet) to international networks (Tennant et al. 1993, 13). In early 1992, the Internet consisted of an estimated 5,000 networks in 33 countries connecting approximately 500,000 computers and as many as three million people (Dern 1992, 111).

The world is in the midst of an information explosion. School library media centers cannot house, nor can they afford to provide, all of the information students need. And yet, in view of greater learning expectations, that is the need—access to a world of information. Today's technology permits learning and the search for information to extend beyond the school walls. The Internet provides an opportunity for global learning, access to almost unlimited information, easy and rapid communication, and technology that captures the interest of both teachers and students.

RESOURCES AVAILABLE ON THE INTERNET

How can the Internet be used to enhance teaching and learning? Most users first become acquainted with electronic mail. It is a popular function of the network, allowing users to communicate with an ease and speed not provided by telephone service or the U.S. Postal Service (so-called "snail mail"). Electronic mail breaks down geographic barriers, allowing users to develop professional contacts around the world in a way that would have previously been difficult if not impossible (Tennant et al. 1993, 39).

The Internet also offers communication access by means of listserv. A user selects a list to which he would like to subscribe. Messages sent to the list are routed to all of the subscribers. Through these lists subscribers can share ideas, ask questions, and keep up-to-date on trends. For example, media specialists who subscribe to LM_NET share concerns about such topics as budgets, censorship, charging fines, networking CD-ROM products, and student access to telecommunications.

There are thousands of lists to which a user can subscribe on any topic imaginable. For example, there is a list for people interested in scholarly discussion of film and television (Screen-L), one for people interested in educational technology (Edtech), another for jazz lovers (JAZZ-L), even one for people interested in vampiric lore (VAMPYRES). There is a list for every conceivable interest, personal or professional. An example of a list to which teachers and media specialists might subscribe is KIDSPHERE. It was created in 1989 under the name KIDSNET with the purpose of stimulating the "development of an international computer network for the use of children and their teachers" (Johnson, M. 1993). IECC (International E-mail Classroom Connections) is another list that might interest teachers. It serves as a meeting place for teachers seeking partner classes for international and cross-cultural mail exchanges.

The Internet also provides access to a world of information through the telnet function. This allows a user to login to computer systems anywhere on the network. Every telnet site has an address that the user uses to connect to the system. The command structure of the remote system is used because the remote system is accessed as if the local terminal were attached directly to it.

Telnet offers an opportunity to access resources on computer networks throughout the world. For example, when a user in Columbia, Missouri, goes online using the local freenet COIN (Columbia Online Information Network), he is able to obtain local information about city, county, and state government; social services agencies; public school schedules; recreational opportunities; public library services; and so on. By accessing the telnet function of the Internet, the COIN user is also able to access the system at the University of California at Santa Cruz (infoslug.ucsc.edu) where he will find, among other resources, the Congressional Directory for the 103rd Congress and the FY95 U.S. budget. He may telnet to Rutgers University (info.rutgers.edu) to find the texts of such historical documents as the Bill of Rights, the Declaration of Independence, and the United States Constitution. Or he could telnet to the community-sponsored Heartland Freenet in Peoria, Illinois (heartland.bradley.edu), where he can locate governmental, educational, recreational, and other types of information specific to that area.

The last of the three functions of the Internet is file transfer protocol, or ftp. Ftp allows the user to move files from a remote computer system to the local system. The process is similar to that of the telnet function: the user specifies an address to connect to the remote system. He then uses the login name "anonymous" and his e-mail address as the password to gain access to the directory from which the desired files can be selected.

SEARCHING THE INTERNET

There is no single guide or directory that is able to list all of the resources available on the Internet. Because of this there are continuing efforts to make the Internet more user-friendly. Jean Armour Polly, author of "Surfing the Internet," describes some of the tools that have been created for this purpose as "travel agents." Their purpose is to give direction and help the user make some sense of the massive amount of information on the Internet (1993). These tools include gopher, WAIS, Veronica, Archie, and World-Wide Web.

The Internet gopher is not a burrowing rodent with wide cheek pouches but something closer to the slang definition of a gopher as someone who runs errands for others. The Internet gopher is a document delivery service. It provides a hierarchical menu system through which the user can select a menu item to lead to the desired text, to another level of menus, or to yet another gopher system. The user is able to browse through a variety of resources on the Internet using the gopher menus.

Wide Area Information Servers, or WAIS, also makes searching easier. The user enters a keyword or group of words and the WAIS searches the Internet archives for articles containing the term(s) (Krol 1992, 211). There is an overwhelming amount of information on the Internet and the main benefit of the WAIS is that it provides an easy search method for navigating the Internet using natural language searches (Lukanuski 1992, 743).

Veronica (Very Easy Rodent-Oriented Net-Wide Index to Computerized Archives) works within the gopher framework. The user enters a keyword search and Veronica does the work, searching through gopher menu files. According to Steve Foster, one of the developers of Veronica, "the result of a Veronica search is an automatically-generated gopher menu, customized according to the user's keyword specification" (Polly 1993).

Archie is a tool for locating files available through anonymous ftp. It allows searching by keyword or by a group of words. Archie then gives the user the actual filenames of the files that match the search as well as the name of the servers where those files are located (Krol 1992, 155).

The World-Wide Web (WWW) is one of the newer information services available on the Internet. It attempts "to organize all the information on the Internet, plus whatever local information you want, as a set of hypertext documents" (Krol 1992, 229). What this means is that the user is able to look at one document and then move to other related documents by means of links.

USING THE INTERNET FOR
TEACHING AND LEARNING

Telecommunications is a valid and powerful tool for learning. Students are able to use the Internet for everything "from researching local history, to learning foreign languages, to understanding global ecology" (Mageau 1990, 26). They can search databases for information or communicate using electronic mail. They can collaborate on projects with students across town or halfway around the world or they can query experts for firsthand information. This type of information provides students with access to the world, offering them "the reality of the global village in personal, hands-on, interactive ways" (Rogers 1994, 28).

How are schools using these resources? Among the thousands of resources available through the Internet, some that may interest K-12 media specialists and teachers include the text of historical documents such as the U.S. Constitution, the CIA World Factbook, weather reports from the National Weather Service, online book reviews, NASA information services, earthquake reports, and databases containing Supreme Court decisions or legislation from the U.S. Congress. There are databases with sports schedules, song lyrics, recipes, census information, tropical storm reports, and even a list of the day's events in history.

Students and teachers are able to use the available information in many different ways. For example, at Hickman High School in Columbia, Missouri, a class of language arts students were given a writing assignment to describe where they would like to live and why. They used the Internet to find census information on unemployment, average income, and housing costs to help determine why one city would be better than another. In another case, a biology teacher wanted to know the status of specific endangered species legislation. The desired information was located in LOCIS (Library of Congress Information System). This resource available through telnet (locis.loc.gov) contains bills and resolutions introduced to Congress, copyright information, and foreign law as well as the Library of Congress catalog.

German teacher Bob Brady was one of the first Hickman teachers to use the Internet with his students. He followed the progress of the German scientists who were aboard a 1993 shuttle flight with the Americans, checking NASA resources such as NASA Spacelink and NASA News daily. His students wanted to know whether the Germans spoke English or German during the shuttle flight. That question was not addressed in the NASA databases. In an effort to find the information he sent an electronic mail message to NASA. They promptly responded with the answer; they spoke English.

The following school year, Brady used electronic mail to conference with German teachers on topics such as violence in schools and to share course information. He also involved his students in collaborative writing projects using electronic mail. They wrote in German to German students in Spokane, Washington, and to German students in the English as a second language program at a college in Vermont.

Teachers and students in Columbia, Missouri's, elementary schools have also used the Internet in a variety of ways in the past two years. Students at Rock Bridge Elementary School in Columbia used resources on the Internet to study the tundra. In addition, they communicated with students in Alaska using electronic mail. They got firsthand information about what it was like to live on the tundra (Matthews 1993, 16A).

Students at another Columbia elementary school participated in a one-day project that involved recording their activities on March 2, 1994. They wrote down they activities at the top of every hour throughout the day. The notes were transferred into a class file and sent by electronic mail to other participating classes worldwide. Students then compared their activities with those of the other classes, listing similarities and differences. Another class participated in a project called "What's for Supper"? They decided on a menu that represented a typical meal for a Midwest family dinner. They sent it to other classes participating in the project. In return they received menus from school children in Germany, France, Spain, and all the regions of the United States.

Phyllis Sallman, media specialist at Columbia's Shepherd Elementary School, introduced COIN and the Internet to her 500 students. She organized and coordinated projects for each grade level, relating each project to an existing curricular unit. For example, second-grade students gathered weather data to share with students in New York; students in third grade corresponded with a class in San Francisco while working on their oceans unit; and, fifth-grade students summarized information obtained while on a field trip to share with a class in New York. The benefits of the telecommunications projects to the Shepherd students were the creation of a global classroom, motivation to learn, a wealth of information and variety of projects, and the opportunity to exchange ideas with other children around the world.

In December 1992, subscribers to LM_NET responded to a request for information about ways in which schools are using telecommunications. Following is a summary of some of the responses (Haynes 1993). Teachers used the Internet to access NASA Spacelink and weather information. Spanish teachers in the same school sent letters written in Spanish to students in El Paso. At a different school, students participated in a cooperative learning venture about water resources with other classes across the state. At another, students were involved in a worldwide project to see how much of a meteor shower could be seen in their part of the world. Students from all over the world set their watches to Greenwich time to be a part of the study. Other students retrieved information about recent earthquakes to make a world map charting them. One individual responding to the survey remarked that her daughter used telecommunications to locate information about university scholarships and grants.

Several Chicago-area school districts participated in a partnership called Project Homeroom with IBM, Illinois Bell, and Ameritech. The purpose of the project was to investigate telephone and computer technology to see how the school day could be extended and the learning process enhanced. Access was provided to national news services, online encyclopedias, science and financial statistics, and the individual school libraries. At home, students could even access their personal work files stored on computers at school. Students were able to communicate with other students and teachers using electronic mail. In some cases, the students were even able to turn in their assignments from their computers at home to the teacher's at school (Ward 1992, A20).

Students at Penn High School in Mishawaka, Indiana, discovered through the Internet that a class in Alaska was working on a project similar to theirs—designing a small submarine. During the course of the project the two classes set up a data link to share strategies and information (Walker 1993, 51).

In *The Chronicle of Higher Education*, Katherine S. Managan describes ways in which public schools and academic institutions are cooperatively using computer networks (1992, A17-18). In Glendora, California, children in the third grade communicated with elementary students in Zimbabwe. They had a firsthand opportunity to learn about their culture, school, and family. The link was arranged by a faculty member at California State Polytechnic University who was conducting research on distance learning. In Vermont, elementary students from several schools worked together to write a geography textbook for young children. The students did the research and then sent the information by network to a central school, which assembled the information and published the book.

Most of the media specialists responding to the LM_NET survey noted that they use electronic mail on a regular basis, both for communication within their districts and for sharing information on the network. Several media specialists indicated that their teachers were interested in features such as AskERIC (a service of the Educational Resources Information Center that allows teachers, administrators, and media specialists to ask questions about education). Within 48 hours they will receive either the answer or instructions about where to find the answer (Johnson, M. 1993). An estimated 50,000 teachers currently use the Internet. The major reasons they give, according to a 1993 survey published by the New York City Bank Street College of Education, are "to expand student awareness about the world, to strengthen students' inquiry-based analytical skills, to communicate with other educators, and to combat professional isolation" (Dyrli 1993, 51).

The above examples are only a few of the ways teachers are using the Internet to enhance learning and teaching by connecting the school with the global community. The possibilities are almost unlimited, as is the information.

Today 20% of all information is available online. By the year 2000, 90% of all information will be available online (Johnson, D. 1993). Access to the vast resource of information provided by the Internet will be essential for teaches and students. This electronic highway will provide the "opportunity for students . . . to move intellectually beyond their own school walls, to take advantage of information that would never before have been available to them" (Dougherty 1991, 43). With a world of information at their fingertips, all students can be global learners.

REFERENCES

Arms, Caroline R. 1990. "A New Information Infrastructure." *Online* (September): 15-22.

Bishop, Anne P. 1990. "The National Research and Education Network (NREN): "Promise of New Information Environments." [Machine-readable data file]. *ERIC Digest* (November). ED 327 219.

Dern, Daniel. 1992. "Applying the Internet." *BYTE* (February): 111-18.

Dougherty, Richard M. 1991. "Pathways to Our Future." *School Library Journal* (February): 43.

Dyrli, Odvard Egil. 1993. "The Internet: Bringing Global Resources to the Classroom." *Technology & Learning* (October): 50-58.

"Educational Technology for K-12" [Electronic mail]. *Congressional Roll Call* 24 (May): 18. LM_NET@SUVM.SYR.EDU

Haynes, Elizabeth. 1993. "Re: Internet Info Responses" [Electronic mail]. (April 12). LM_NET@SUVMSYREDU. 14:49 cst.

Johnson, Doug. 1993. "New Roles for School Media Specialists" [Electronic mail]. (April 10). LM_NET@SUVM.SYR.EDU. 11:22 cst.

Johnson, Madeline. 1993. "Name Change: KIDSNET—KIDSPHERE" [Electronic mail]. LM_NET@SUVM.SYR.EDU. 17:39.

Krol, Ed. 1992. *The Whole Internet User's Guide and Catalog.* Sebastopol, CA: O'Reilly, 1992.

Lukanuski, Mary. 1992. "Help Is on the WAIS." *American Libraries* (October): 742-44.

Mageau, Therese. 1990. "Teaching and Learning Online." *Electronic Learning* (November/ December): 26-30.

Managan, Katherine S. 1992. "Computer Networks Help Public Schools Forge New Ties with Higher Education." *The Chronicle of Higher Education* 9 (September): A17-18.

Matthews, Gregory. 1993. "COIN Opens Window on World." *Columbia Missourian* 2 (June): 16A.

Noonan, Dana. 1992. *A Guide to Internet/Bitnet* [Machine-readable data file]. (June). Metropolitan State University, METRONET.

Polly, Jean Armour. 1993. "Surfing the Internet: An Introduction" [Machine-readable data file], Version 2. (April 26). UC Santa Cruz InfoSlug System, 12:08.

Rogers, Al. 1994. "Living the Global Village." *Electronic Learning* (May/June): 28-29.

Tennant, Roy, John Ober, and Anne G. Lipow. *Crossing the Internet Threshold: An Instructional Handbook.* Berkeley, CA: Library Solutions Press, 1993.

Walker, Michael. 1993. "Space-Age Schools: Techno Wonders Are Changing the Way Our Children Learn." *Better Homes and Gardens* (May).

Ward, Ann. 1992. "Putting Telecommunications to Work." *The Electronic School* (September): A16-21.

3

LM_NET
Helping School Library Media Specialists to Shape the Networking Revolution in the Schools

MICHAEL B. EISENBERG and PETER MILBURY

The Internet, the electronic superhighway, the new revolution in tele-communications—it's being talked about everywhere, from the mass media to professional journals to the White House. This is it: The latest wave of technological and related social change is upon us. And of course, these developments portend much for the future of education. For library media professionals the question is, Where are we in all this? Is the situation similar to past waves that, at best, just swept us along or, at worst, just swept on by? No, this time it's different. This time school library media specialists are right out in front, riding the wave, making it happen.

The Internet is the network of networks, linking computer users throughout the world with one another and with a dazzling variety of resources. This alone should be enough to effect major changes in schools and libraries. But, the Internet does more than simply provide access to a world of databases and technological resources. The Internet brings a human dimension to technology through its ability to connect widely separated individuals. Internet users contact each other via electronic mail. They also hold group conversations through specialized electronic discussion groups. In a few enviable situations, remote Internet users find themselves in a "virtual community," one that breaks down professional isolation and supports cooperation, innovation, and new ideas.

For school library media specialists, LM_NET, the electronic discussion group for people interested in or involved in school library media work, represents such a virtual community. The term *community* is not used lightly. There are thousands of electronic bulletin boards and Internet listservs (i.e., electronic discussion groups). LM_NET did start out, in June 1992, as "one more" electronic forum. But, it quickly evolved into something much more than a means for communicating information and ideas. Perhaps this is due to its role in breaking the isolation of school library media specialists (often there is only one in any given school), or maybe this is because school library media professionals are quick to embrace and effectively use

29

new technologies. Whatever the reasons, LM_NET can truly be described as a virtual community: a cohesive group of widely dispersed people who hold common interests, help one another share problems and solutions, and work together to fulfill individual and group goals through the use of e-mail and other electronic communication tools.

Though the Internet and LM_NET may be revolutionary in their potential for changing the way library media specialists are perceived as well as the way they fulfill their roles, both also build upon a history of technological innovations dating to the mid-1960s. At that time, with the infusion of financial support from the Elementary and Secondary Education Act, school libraries began to evolve into media centers. Ten years later, it was common to find not only filmstrips, audiocassettes, and microfiche as part of the school library, but also graphic, photographic, audio, and television production capabilities. The eighties brought the computer, and library media programs began to offer automated circulation and catalog services. The decade spilled into the 1990s on the rallying cry of "Information Power" with a proactive vision supported by new opportunities for offering electronic databases and resources on CD-ROMs and local area networks.

From this point, it was a small step technologically (but a great leap conceptually) to global connectivity. Adding modems and communications capabilities allowed library media specialists to connect to regional wide area networks, which, in turn, offered gateways to the global Internet. Library media specialists quickly joined the growing numbers of groups and individuals with access to electronic mail and various network resources, retrieval tools, and utilities. Library media specialists were also among the first K-12 educators to see the potential of the network, to explore its capabilities, and to assume a leadership role in bringing connections to their schools. It was only logical for library media specialists to look to the network as a means to support these efforts, and one of the best ways to communicate and share information on the Internet is through an electronic discussion group. And so, this led to formation of the LM_NET.

Less than two years old, LM_NET is already a strong force on the Internet and in the library media profession. With well over 1,000 active participants and hundreds of others "listening in," LM_NET is the focal point for networking activity by library media specialists. The remainder of this article explains exactly what this means by offering:

1. some basics on the technology that supports LM_NET,

2. a brief history of LM_NET development,

3. LM_NET purpose and use,

4. a profile of the LM_NET community,

5. an analysis of LM_NET discussions,

6. special LM_NET features, and

7. a glimpse of the future.

LM_NET TECHNOLOGY

Many library professionals are now familiar with local area networks (LANs), which connect computers and other equipment together within a local setting. There is another form of networking that is sweeping the world: wide area networks (also called WANs). The purpose of wide area networking is to link geographically remote computers in a particular region together so that users can quickly and easily communicate with other users and share information resources on that network.

There are many different options for wide area networking, including local bulletin board systems that are linked together, and commercial services like CompuServe, Prodigy, and America Online. However, the most widespread wide area network, sometimes called the "network of networks," is the Internet. By linking various WANs and other networks and providing standards for communication and resource sharing, the Internet makes it possible for millions of users, who connect through thousands of computer systems, to interact with one another around the world.

Participating in electronic discussion groups (also called listservs) is an important option available to people connected to the Internet. There are thousands of electronic discussion groups on the Internet, ranging from such topics as animal rights to gardening to zoological studies. For education as well, there are numerous listservs. Educators can connect to discussions on administration, counseling, policy, and the use of the Internet for teaching and learning. And students can subscribe to listservs that promote global interaction with other students for specific subjects or just for fun.

Subscribing to a listserv is free and relatively easy—if someone is already connected to the Internet.[1] Once subscribed, a user will receive every message that is sent to the computer upon which the listserv software is located. This is because, unlike electronic bulletin boards, which require users to ask to see posted messages, listservs work by re-sending posted messages to every subscriber. So, if someone signs up to many discussion groups, he or she can receive hundreds of messages every day!

The capabilities of the Internet and listservs are the foundation for LM_NET. Anyone with access to the Internet and interested in the school library media field can sign up by sending an e-mail request to: listserv@listserv.syr.edu. In the body of your message simply state: subscribe lm_net firstname lastname.

LM_NET: A BRIEF HISTORY

The idea of a discussion group for school library media professionals on the Internet was first raised by Mike Eisenberg (Professor at the School of Information Studies, Syracuse University, and Director of the ERIC Clearinghouse on Information & Technology) in the spring of 1992 with Ann Weeks (Executive Director of the American Association of School Librarians). They immediately agreed that it was a good idea. Eisenberg arranged with Academic Computing Services at Syracuse to set up the necessary listserv software on the Syracuse University mainframe computer.

LM_NET officially began on Friday, June 5, 1992. The original 42 LM_NET members who were placed on the list by Eisenberg were local library media specialists in the Central New York area, Eisenberg's colleagues at different universities, and some New England library media people whose names were sent to Eisenberg by Carolyn Markuson, a well-known library media professional from Massachusetts.

Markuson also told Eisenberg about Peter Milbury, school librarian at Pleasant Valley High School, in Chico, California. During the prior year, Milbury had created an electronically connected group within his e-mail system, using it to communicate with other school librarians. This "Leading Edge Librarians" group, as Milbury had optimistically dubbed it, was composed of Milbury's local colleagues, others who had attended his conference workshops, and others whom Milbury had come across through postings to other education-oriented Internet discussion groups or had been referred by others in his e-mail group. Eisenberg and Milbury began to communicate with each other on June 8, and Milbury was added as co-owner of LM_NET on June 15. The next day, Milbury's "Leading Edge Librarians" (most from California) were officially merged with the existing LM_NET list, bringing the membership close to 100. LM_NET grew steadily over the summer with information spreading through workshops, word-of-mouth, postings to various library-related or education-related Internet discussion groups, and brief articles in newsletters and journals. During July, 12 members met for the very first LM_NET in-person gathering, held at the ALA Conference in San Francisco.

By September, there were 250 LM_NET members, and the number reached 400 by the end of 1992. Following publicity in two national journals in January 1993, over 100 new members were added by the first of February. Other articles and "media mentions" of LM_NET appeared throughout the year. At the one-year anniversary (June 1993) there were almost 1,000 subscribers, and by the end of the year the list topped 1,300.

LM_NET messages are electronically archived, and any person with Internet access is able to log on to the AskERIC Gopher server and read them (see appendix 3.A, page 47). LM_NET messages are also re-posted to electronic bulletin boards and conference archives on host computers and networks worldwide. More information on this is provided in "A Profile of the LM_NET Community" on page 34.

LM_NET: PURPOSE AND USE

As envisioned by Eisenberg, Weeks, and Milbury, LM_NET was formed to help library media professionals make better use of the services and resources of the Internet and to help them fulfill library media functions. Instructions to new subscribers state:

A FRIENDLY REMINDER: Conversation on LM_NET should focus on the topics of interest to the school library media community, including the latest on school library media services, operations, and activities. It is a list for practitioners helping practitioners, sharing ideas, solving problems, telling each other about new publications and up-coming conferences, asking for assistance or information, and linking schools through their library media centers.

LM_NET is open to all school library media specialists worldwide and people involved with the school library media field. However, LM_NET is *not* for general librarians or educators. We want to keep the activity and discussion focused on school library media.

It is clear that LM_NET has been used for many purposes. Recent examples of use include requests for recommendations for purchase of books and material for the library collection; questions about applications of new technology to the library; announcements and discussions regarding resources available on the Internet; issues and problems related to the profession; planning for get-togethers at regional and national conferences; reference and other assistance to students, teachers, and staff; and administration and policies of library media centers.

As stated at the beginning of this chapter, LM_NET is more than just an electronic discussion group—LM_NET is a community. For example, LM_NETTERS attending the 1993 ALA mid-winter meeting in Denver met and verified the importance of LM_NET in the daily professional lives of practitioners, library educators, and students in library media preparation programs. They discussed how

- LM_NET overcomes isolation by linking even the most remote library media specialist to colleagues throughout the world. Building-level practitioners are able to raise questions and discuss concerns with peers on a regular basis, as if they were in the same setting.

- LM_NET brings practice into the classroom of library media training programs. Already, library educators use the interactions on LM_NET as case studies of real events in real library media settings.

- LM_NET provides easy and open interaction between library media educators and researchers, those in professional leadership positions, and those on the "front lines." This helps bridge the often-expressed gap between theory and practice.

- LM_NET helps develop technology skills among library media specialists. The discussion group allows people to raise technology-related questions and provides information and assistance in using the Internet as well as other technologies.

- LM_NET creates a sense of belonging. Library media professionals and others involved in the field have a "home on the Internet" that is targeted specifically at their interests.

- LM_NET puts the library media profession into the center of the national networking movement. In many ways, the interactions and special efforts associated with LM_NET represent cutting-edge applications of listserv and Internet capabilities to professional practice.

Further discussion of specific uses of LM_NET use is offered in "An Analysis of LM_NET Discussions" on page 35.

A PROFILE OF THE
LM_NET COMMUNITY

The LM_NET membership list includes many addresses that represent far more than single e-mail addresses to which messages are sent. These addresses are actually bulletin board systems (BBS) or similar services, which re-post LM_NET postings to their subscribers. Typically, this is a wide area network (WAN) such as Florida's FIRN, North Dakota's SENDIT BBS, Texas's TENET, or the international FidoNet echo, FrEdMail.

The LM_NET e-mail address list also includes addresses that account for re-postings to college and university networks, such as Western Carolina University's MicroNet, the University of Massachusetts's UMassK12 BBS, the University of Kentucky's Netnews redistribution. They range beyond the U.S. borders, from an informal re-posting by a school librarian for 18 senior high library colleagues in Alberta, Canada, to Australia's FidoNet Gateway and the Australia Librarians BBS, to organizations such as the Health Sciences Libraries Consortium (and a number of others around the world).

One of the goals of the LM_NET owners was that it be open to school librarians from other countries, thus taking full advantage of the global Internet. By December 3, 1992, when LM_NET was almost six months old, there were 400 members from 6 countries. A year later, by December 1993, there were over 1,200 members from 15 countries. (See table 3.1.) Currently, 91 percent of the members come from the United States. These U.S. members are widely dispersed, with the largest numbers coming from the states of Texas, New York, California, Pennsylvania, Massachusetts, Minnesota, Florida, and Virginia.

Table 3.1. Growth and Distribution of LM_NET Membership

Membership in December 1992	Membership in December 1993
390 U.S.A.	1,162 U.S.A.
6 Canada	54 Canada
1 Belgium	12 Australia
1 Germany	3 Iceland
1 Finland	2 Czech Republic
1 New Zealand	2 Finland
	2 Japan
	2 New Zealand
	1 Belgium
	1 Colombia
	1 Great Britain
	1 Italy
	1 Malaysia
	1 Netherlands
	1 Singapore
	27 Unknown

An analysis of LM_NET membership by Dr. Anne Clyde[2] found that by October 1, 1993, the 1,137 members on LM_NET accessed the Internet via 363 different host computers or networks. Dr. Clyde found that LM_NET is "a very dispersed group, both geographically and in terms of the hosts used." There were 45 hosts used by 5 or more LM_NET members, and these 45 accounted for approximately 60 percent of the membership. Clyde also found that the Texas network, TENET, hosted the largest number of LM_NET members (119, or 10 percent). California is second with 71 subscribers through the CALSTATE node.

AN ANALYSIS OF
LM_NET DISCUSSIONS

A descriptive analysis of LM_NET message postings reveals some interesting patterns. (See table 3.2.) The typical number of messages posted to LM_NET daily grew from 6 to 19 during 1993. December was likely affected by vacation and time constraints. The growth of messages seems to be directly proportional to growth in membership as the number of messages doubled while the membership more than tripled.

Table 3.2. Analysis of 1993 LM_NET Message Postings

Month	# Message Postings	Daily Average	Avg. # of Members
January	181	06	502
February	337	12	601
March	413	13	700
April	276	09	795
May	389	13	860
June	277	09	940
July	355	11	1,020
August	298	10	1,078
September	493	16	1,120
October	594	19	1,215
November	569	19	1,265
December	494	16	1,269

Postings to LM_NET for May 1993 were analyzed to see if LM_NET was dominated by any individuals or groups of individuals. Most of the LM_NET messages were posted by users who sent five messages or fewer during the period. In May 1993, 108 (91 percent) of the users accounted for 182 (65 percent) of the messages. This particular posting of messages seems more widespread than the 20-80 relationship often cited for library use (i.e., where the top 20 percent of active users account for 80 percent of the questions, and 80 percent of the users account for only 20 percent of the use). In May 1993 for LM_NET, 20 percent (24) of the active users do account for 67 percent (189) of the questions, but 84 percent (100) of the users account for 52 percent (147) of the postings. In addition, other than the LM_NET coordinator, no one posted more than 10 messages.[3] One disappointment was the percentage of total membership posting to LM_NET. Only 14 percent (119) of the 860 members participated actively in LM_NET during May.

A broad content analysis was conducted of postings to LM_NET during November 1993. There was a total of 569 messages posted during the month. These messages seemed to fall into eight categories. (See table 3.3.) Specific examples of messages (some have been edited) are presented below, grouped according to the eight categories outlined in the table. Together, the set of exchanges shows the diversity of LM_NET discussion. The messages also demonstrate how an electronic community offers a new and powerful approach to information seeking for questions related to library media as well as general education.

Table 3.3. Analysis of LM_NET Postings

Posting content categories	Number	Percent
1. Library, school, and district policies, practices, and procedures	146	26
2. Location and use of Internet resources	94	17
3. Reference questions directed to teachers and others	88	15
4. Products and resources for the library collection	85	15
5. General discussion of librarianship issues	65	11
6. Training tips and software use	51	9
7. LM_NET administration and use	22	4
8. Workshop and conference announcements/ discussion	18	3

Category 1. Library, school, and district policies, practices, and procedures

Posting: Our 7-12 rural high school in VT is exploring outcomes based programs ("outcomes" seems to be a dirty word, so my principal prefers "standards-based education" or exit skills). How do library/information skills figure into such a program, if your school uses an outcomes-based model? Mary Powers, Vermont

Response: An American Assn of School Librarians committee was formed to focus on "Outcome-Based Education" and is working on a position statement. At the Midwinter meeting it will be revised enough to publish, I believe, and I can get you a copy. In the meantime I have TONS of stuff about OBE. You should especially look at California Media and Library Educators stuff on "Information Literacy." Its POWERFUL!! Debbie Abilock

Posting: Hi HS Media Generalists. I need your assistance concerning how your students gain entrance to your lmc. *do they come in on a pass from a study hall teacher, subject teacher, or on a pass from you?? Lynne Jackson

Response: So far, our students have open access. The problem was that we have so many students coming to the library (yea!) that teachers would come and ask if the students they allowed to come got there. Betty Hamilton

Posting: Should I create brief circulation records for each magazine title in our holdings (microform, cd, and all) so that they will get the full treatment in the opac? Shelley Lochhead

Response: I speak as one who has supervised or conducted 27 retros. . . . My recommendation: Buy the serials control module of your automation package. Not only will it have a means to provide online access to your serials, it will also maintain issue-by-issue histories, project due dates for future issues, and print and track claim letters. It MAY also provide routing and table of contents listings, as well. For elementary schools, this is overkill; but for high schools which subscribe to almost 100 titles, this is a godsend! Carol Mann Simpson

Category 2. Location and use of Internet resources

Posting: My school district is looking at various possibilities for Internet access for our teachers and students. . . . We are curious about what other schools do to provide Internet access. We would like to hear from you about how you get on the net. We are interested in using e-mail, telnet, Gopher, ftp. Thanks! Patricia Gosda

Response: Our teachers and students can get accounts on CORE, our California educational net that provides Internet access. . . . So far, we have not had problems with misuse. The phone call to access CORE is a local phone call, so no toll charges are involved. Students and faculty can access CORE from either school computers with modems or home computers. We feel very fortunate to have this kind of access. Marge Cargo

(Note: The following message was posted as a follow-up by its author, who had earlier requested recommendations for Internet resources.)

Posting: Thanks to all who responded with suggestions . . . My original message asked for opinions as to the top 5 Internet resources to demo to secondary school librarians/administrators considering the provision of student access to the Internet. I tried all the resources suggested to me; here is my top 5 list.

1. KUfacts (my contribution) telnet to ukanaix.cc.ukans.edu, login kufacts

2. AskERIC telnet to ericir.syr.edu login Gopher

3. LOCIS telnet to locis.loc.gov

4. WASHLAW telnet to acc.wuacc.edu login washlaw

5. Victoria Free-Net telnet to freenet.victoria.bc.ca login guest

Best of luck to all you Internet trainers!! Bruce Flanders

Category 3. Reference questions directed to teachers and others

Posting: Our 7th grade Industrial Technology teacher is looking for a CAD program for use on a Macintosh that will allow students to design projects that they will eventually construct from paper, cardboard, or wood. I don't think he is looking for anything too sophisticated, just user friendly and does the job. Ross Boehm

Response: Our 7th and 8th graders use the draw layer of Superpaint. It isn't anything special, but it does the job and is fairly easy to use.   Steve Baule

Posting: We are looking for explanations of the stock market for high school students. Any suggestions. It seems to me there ought to be some free and/or inexpensive material out there.   Jacqueline Van Willigen

Response: I don't know about free and/or expensive materials, but there is a stock market game run out of New Mexico State University in Las Cruces. Several of our economics teachers utilize having students play and playing themselves. You do have to pay to mail your students' activities reports. The teachers find it very beneficial for themselves and the students. Bel Air High School is 98 percent Hispanic and low income students who know that information is power. Diana Kisselburg

Posting: A staff member has requested titles of good stories, myths, legends dealing with EARLY MAN/PEOPLE. She would like to use Story as way of teaching her Social Studies program this year.   Chuck Heath

Response: How about THE LEGEND OF THE CRANBERRY; A PALEO-INDIAN TALE by Ellin Greene, Illus by Brad Sneed. (Simon & Schuster, 1993). Legend in which the Great Spirit gave the world the cranberry to remind people of their great battle with the mastedons and woolly mammoths . . . appropriate for the holidays, too.   Debbie Abilock

Category 4. Products and resources for the library collection

Posting: I discovered (my second year here—I'm still learning the collection) this book on our shelves today, "Faithful Elephants: A True Story of Animals, People, and War" and was in tears by the time I finished it. It's a very moving story about three elephants who were starved to death at the Ueno Zoo in Tokyo during WWII. A decision had been made to kill all the zoo's animals in case bombs hit the city and the animals got loose, and other methods failed when they tried to kill the elephants more mercifully. My question is: the intro, the title, everything says this is a true story, but the CIP puts the book in fiction. Is it indeed true? . . . Is the Ueno Zoo still there? The book was first published in Japan in 1951 and translated and illustrated in 1988.   Pat Heydweiller

Response: I have just read your e-mail at the university terminal in Tokyo. Right now I can only answer to the latter part of your question, that is, the Ueno Zoo still exists which is the largest zoo in Japan and yes, we killed many wild big animals during the war. Not only dangerous when air raids hit here but also there was not much food to feed them. For the rest of your question, I will try to find out.   Setsuko Koga

Category 5. General discussion of librarianship issues

Posting: Hello, I'm a grad student doing an issues project on the issue of library cooperation between the public library and the elementary library. . . . I would like suggestions from anyone dealing with issues like budgeting, roles of the media specialist, security, space, and administrative issues. I would love to hear from any school that houses a public library. Please give me your best pros and cons. Thanks for your help!   Jim Schick

Response: There are many advantages to school and public library cooperation—for all of the partners—and many of these are articulated in the research summaries in WHAT WORKS; RESEARCH ABOUT TEACHING AND LEARNING THROUGH THE SCHOOL'S LIBRARY RESOURCE CENTER [Rockland Press, 1992]. There are also many specific examples of types of cooperation [see for example, *Emergency Librarian*, 16:5 (1989 May-June), pp. 27-30]. The issue is not whether one is in favor or not. The issue is what criteria have been established to ensure a better chance for success of such an operation? These are outlined in *Emergency Librarian*, 17 :4 (1990, March-April), pp. 33-34. This is another one of those issues in teacher-librarianship where the research and expert opinion converge but every decade or so it appears as another emotional rendition. The writings of Aaron and Amey [and Haycock] are instructive, among others.   Ken Haycock

Posting: A few weeks ago I sent a message about the possibility of Chapter II funds being eliminated. The possibility still exists!! Congress will not get around to this legislation until after the Christmas Recess, because of NAFTA and Health Care. We still need letters sent to the President, Rep. Dale Kildee, Senator Edward Kennedy and Secretary of Education Richard Riley!!!

The President has an Internet address, but only a few members of Congress have Internet addresses. Please write and visit your local Congress members and Senators during the recess between Thanksgiving and Christmas, when they will be home!!!   Tom Hart

Category 6. Training tips and software use

Posting: Does anyone out there have any suggestions for software to allow MACs to print out DOS files? All our CD-ROMs in the library are MS-DOS and the students would like to save to disk and print out later in the MACs in the computer lab.   Alicia Astorga

Response: If the file exchange was not originally installed with your System 7, you can find it on the disk Tidbits.   Ross Boehm

Posting: How do you handle virus control in your computers? Our school computers were infected with the "tequila" virus last week and played havoc with our operation. . . . Does anyone know exactly how the tequila virus affects a program; and what is your method of ensuring a virusfree environment?   Betty Dawn Hamilton

Response: Every computer you own should have a virus protection system installed. It's really the only way to practice safe computing. If your school can't afford one of the commercial versions such as Virex, then there are several Freeware virus protectors such as Disinfectant. Disinfectant is available on the net and can be downloaded from several sites.   John See

Category 7. LM_NET administration and use

Posting: Dear LM_NET Members,
In case anyone is wondering what the TARGET-> talk is all about, you might like to read the following.

* * *Using the TARGET-> discussion process, a friendly reminder. TARGET-> is a fourstep process:

1. The TARGET-> originator proposes the subject for answering/commenting.

2. Those interested in the subject send their responses to the originator of the TARGET-> question. Please do NOT post the response to the group.

3. TARGET-> originator summarizes or collates the responses, and then,

4. Posts the summarized responses to the entire list, using the original TARGET-> Subject in the subject of their message.

The TARGET-> approach is particularly effective when someone has a specific question that needs a variety of suggestions, experiences, practices or sources. It is not always appropriate. The intent of TARGET-> is to make LM_NET more valuable to its growing list of members. Thank you for your support of this innovation in Internet discussions.   Peter Milbury, for LM_NET

Posting: Netters, Did someone ask questions about a four period day a while back? If so, I would really like any summary of the advantages and disadvantages you may have received. This is to provide some info for our staff development coordinator. Thanks.   David Sparks, Minnesota

Posting: Dear LM_NET Colleagues,
If you missed saving an important LM_NET message, all is not lost. They are stored in the LM_NET Archives, at AskERIC. You can find them by following the instructions below.

LM_NET ARCHIVES NOW AVAILABLE BY GOPHER

The LM_NET Archives are now available at the AskERIC Gopher site. The quickest way to find them is to use Telnet to go to a Gopher server, and then, by going through a series of menus, you will reach the LM_NET Archives, at the AskERIC (ERIC-IR) Gopher.

For example: Telnet to a Gopher server on the Internet, as in the following:

1. Telnet to> consultant.micro.umn.edu (or other Gopher address)

2. At the login prompt, type: Gopher (or other specified login)

3. At the TERM=(vt100) prompt, press: return key (or enter your terminal type)

4. LM_NET is found by moving through the following directories, which are given as menu choices through the main Gopher menu.   Peter G. Milbury

Category 8. Workshop and conference announcements/discussion

Posting: The Young Adult Library Services Association (YALSA), a division of the American Library Association (ALA), has established a Young Adult Literature Discussion Group. The group is designed for YALSA members who teach young adult literature and/or are interested in teaching literature for young adults as an opportunity to exchange ideas, course syllabi and information about young adult literature. The first meeting of the discussion group will be held on Sunday, February 6, 1994, 4:30 to 5:30p.m., during the ALA Midwinter Meeting in Los Angeles. For more information, contact the YALSA Office, 800-545-2433, ext. 4390.   Merri M Monks

Posting: Good morning from LA! It's a comfortable day here at the ALA conference. Just seeing bare ground is a treat for someone from Syracuse. The LM_NET breakfast was held this morning. A packed house! Thanks to Ann S. for use of her suite. There was lots of energy and talk and good will—just like LM_NET! The best part for me was meeting so many new people and putting faces with userids. For example, I finally got to meet Mel Roseman. He's as terrific and facilitiating in person as he is on the net. There was no agenda or formal meeting here—just interchange. Many of us seem to agree that it's crucial we keep LM_NET flexible, open, and unstructured. Seems like there's a whole lot of other efforts to provide structure (and control?), so we'll just jump in with a little chaos. That's about it. . . . We are already planning another breakfast for Miami and a get together in Indiana (for AASL) in the Fall as well. Also, stay tuned for immediate announcements of award winners . . . posted on LM_NET first, I can assure you.

Warm regards to all LM_NETTERS from me and the entire LM_NET group here at ALA . . . to making a better world.   Mike Eisenberg

Response[1]: Writing from the Internet Room at the ALA Exhibit area of the L.A. Convention Center, I am thrilled at having met everyone who came to the breakfast this morning. I feel that I am truly an honorary Library/Media teacher.

I have written in the past about LM_NET being a community as well as an information service. It was therefore not surprising that many of us recognized each other *without* looking at name tags. Mike Eisenberg is as vital and energetic in person as he is in cyberspace; the rest of us, both those who write and those who lurk, are equally dedicated to giving students access to the considerable, growing Internet resources.   Mel Roseman, California

Response[2]: I agree, Mike, LM_NET is a helpful line out into the world because of the flexibility and freedom of use. I am a new school librarian, actually this is my second year, but there seems to be millions of things to learn especially with the tech. changes. I find LM_NET keeps me aware of current changes to which I would never be exposed with just the printed page of journals. The people seem so R E A L.   Carol Brown, Arkansas

As one can see, the wide range of discussions, announcements, questions, and answers serve the LM_NET community in many different ways. It provides a very rich tapestry of many different threads, each of which weaves LM_NET members into a virtual community that provides not only information, but support, friendship, and comfort as well. The next section will examine several of the special features that add value to this community.

SPECIAL VALUE-ADDED FEATURES OF LM_NET

The success of LM_NET is also due, in part, to a number of value-added features that have been developed by the co-owners and several active members of LM_NET. These features are 1) mentoring, 2) monitoring, 3) a directory of mentors, 4) archives, and 5) daily digests.

LM_NET Mentoring

The LM_NET community strives to provide support for members whenever possible. One unique project that exemplifies this effort is the LM_NET mentoring program, known as the Telecommunications Skills Index. Shelley Lochhead, from New Hampshire, coordinates this program that links experienced LM_NET network users with new members who need additional assistance in using the full range of Internet services and resources. As explained by Lochhead in her posting to LM_NET members: "In the interests of helping our members become brave and independent surfers on the InterNet, LM_Net sponsors this skills index. Here you will find the names and e-mail addresses of kindly folks who have volunteered to field questions in areas of their telecommunications expertise."

The following outline of support services shows an extensive variety of areas of expertise available through the Telecommunications Skills Index.

Part One: The Basics—tips on getting help, telecommunications software (by type and platform), UNIX, VMS, regional networks (by network).

Part Two: Internet Tools—Archie, e-mail, Gopher, listserv, telnet, UseNet News, VERONICA, WAIS, WorldWideWeb (WWW).

For information on the resources and people available to help you, please obtain the Telecommunications Skills Index file, stored in the LM_NET file list with the name SKILLS INDEX. Anyone can fetch a copy at any time by sending getskills index lm_net by e-mail to listserv@listserv.syr.edu (or to listserv@suvm, for BITNET users).

LM_NET Monitoring

The "Internet monitoring program" is another effort to provide special services to LM_NET members. Here, various LM_NET members agree to monitor discussions on other discussion groups and to repost to LM_NET those messages and resources that may be particularly useful to those in the school library media area. This can save hours of effort for the individual LM_NET member. According to the description of this service to new LM_NET members,

LM_NET MONITORS OTHER RELATED LISTSERV DISCUSSION GROUPS   In order to enable LM_NET members benefit from important information which may be posted to other listserv discussion groups with related interests, a number of members are actively monitoring various lists and information sources. When useful messages and information is found, it is reposted to LM_NET. The need to subscribe to several libraryoriented lists is thereby lessened. Some of the lists and resources currently monitored are: MEDIA-L, HYPERCRD, CoSN, EdTech, Kidsnet, CDROMLAN, CNI-Copyright, Publit. COSN, Internet Hunt Announcement and Results, PACS-L, ALA Feminist Task Force, EDNET, Hilites/NIC.CerfNet, CARRL (Journalism list), and NEWLIST-L.

The LM_NET Directory of Members

Another useful LM_NET membership feature is the "LM_NET Directory of Members," accessible on the AskERIC Gopher site along with the LM_NET Archives. Members volunteer to be listed on this directory, which is maintained and updated by LM_NET member Betty Hamilton. Members are periodically surveyed to provide their name, title/position, institution and its address, telephone and fax numbers, institution's grade levels, professional memberships, and special interests.

LM_NET Archives

The benefits of using the information in LM_NET discussions are not limited to those who are members of the list. Messages are electronically archived and publicly accessible through the AskERIC Gopher server, maintained by the ERIC Clearinghouse on Information and Technology at Syracuse University (see appendix 3.A, page 47). Any person with Internet access is able to log on to the AskERIC Gopher server. Currently, access to the archives is limited to a Gopher menu approach. That is, the messages are stored by month and accessible by title. AskERIC is working on a keyword searching approach to provide an alternative means of access.

The following is an example of what one screen of message titles looks like to a user of the LM_NET Archives on the AskERIC Gopher.

Internet Gopher Information Client 2.0 p 10

Oct_1993

487. Help me access USC online catalog, please.

488. Re: DeskJet Cartridges.

489. LM_NET Digest - Oct 25, 93 - Special issue.

490. E-mail to students at UBVM.

491. Re: Banned books.

492. No Subject.

493. Censorship.

494. Specific E-mail Address Request.

495. Re: Banned books.

496. SOFTWARE QUERY.

497. Information Power.

498. Information Power revisions.

499. Internet access K-12.

500. READERS GUIDE ON CD-ROM.

501. Databases in Schools.

502. No Subject.

503. Re: Democracy.

504. Re: Information Power Revision.

LM_NET Daily Digests

One of the most common complaints regarding Internet use in general and listserv subscription specifically is the problem of message overload. Often, there are simply too many messages for a person to be able to handle. A solution available for LM_NET subscribers is the "digest" option. Instead of receiving messages one at a time from LM_NET, a subscriber can choose to receive messages posted to LM_NET compiled into a grouped message. The subscriber still receives the full, unedited text of all LM_NET exchanges, but clustered together, not one at a time. This eases the number of individual e-mail messages received. While some members say that receiving mail as a digest detracts from the spontaneity of the correspondence, others feel that the cutdown in traffic is more than compensatory. The option is simply one of personal preference.

To activate the digest function, simply send set lm_net digest by e-mail to listserv@suvm.syr.edu. To go back to receiving individual messages, simply send set lm_net mail to listserv@listserv.syr.edu.

LM_NET AND THE FUTURE

Though LM_NET is clearly a success, there is still much to look forward to. First and foremost is the expansion of the membership to a greater percentage of the library media community. There are approximately 70,000 library media professionals in the United States. LM_NET can be used to promote Internet use among library media specialists as well as help various regions gain or improve their access. The LM_NET community will also look to expand its international contacts.

Of course, certain problems and challenges come with expanded membership and size. The most obvious concern is the number of messages posted in a given day. If LM_NET is averaging 19 to 20 messages a day right now, what will happen when the membership increases tenfold? This may require spin-off discussion groups that are coordinated with LM_NET but handle much of the subject-specific traffic. Posting certain types of information in a bulletin board form might also ease the congestion. The key is to retain the positive community attributes without requiring hours of participation each day. We also want to avoid fragmenting the community into subgroups. One of the strengths of LM_NET is its ability to bring together the entire library media profession.

Immediate plans also call for improving access to LM_NET discussions and back files. The ERIC Clearinghouse on Information & Technology (ERIC/IT) at Syracuse will continue to make past LM_NET messages available through a number of different Internet information retrieval systems (e.g., Gopher, FTP, and WAIS). LM_NET will also work with ERIC/IT and other sites to promote improved access through electronic and print help sheets and more user-friendly interfaces (e.g., menu-driven and graphic).

LM_NET will also use its influence to help shape the overall national networking effort, particularly as it relates to K-12 networking. The Clinton administration is committed to establishing a national electronic superhighway. The proposed National Research and Education Network (NREN) is a first step in this effort. It is essential that the nation's schools are a major part of these developments. Furthermore, as the information professionals in schools, library media specialists must play a key role in implementing and using national networks in education. As a unified community, LM_NET will promote K-12 networking and a central role for library media professionals. LM_NET also provides the means for library media specialists to work together to explore the possibilities and fulfill this exciting role.

In summary, LM_NET is already one of the most successful listservs on the Internet. The quality of the discussions, the willingness of members to go out of their way to help each other, and the range of special features separate LM_NET from many other listservs. As technologies evolve, so will the mechanisms and features of LM_NET interaction. However, the baseline has been established. The library media profession now has an active, vibrant electronic side: LM_NET, the electronic library media community. LM_NET will play an increasingly important role in helping library media specialists fulfill their professional responsibilities of providing learning opportunities and services to students and educators.

NOTES

1. At this point in time, gaining Internet access is still not easy for everyone. Various state, regional, and local agencies are working on hooking up their constituents. Other options include a range of commercial service providers. If you do not currently have Internet access, we suggest you investigate options through your local and state education agencies, professional library and educational technology associations, various commercial network service providers, and numerous articles in the library and educational technology literatures.

2. Anne Clyde. "WHO ARE WE?" message posted to LM_NET, Oct. 14, 1993, anne@rhi.hi.is.

3. There were 26 messages posted by the managers of LM_NET. These were primarily informative messages, dealing with new services or features of the list operation (archives, Target->, reminders regarding summer mail suspension, etc.) plus messages forwarded by members who were having trouble posting their own.

APPENDIX 3.A
AskERIC

The AskERIC Project
November 1, 1993

INTRODUCTION

AskERIC is a network-based, human-mediated question answering, help, and referral service for K-12 educators. Begun in November, 1992, by the ERIC Clearinghouse on Information & Technology (ERIC/IT), AskERIC aims to help teachers, library media specialists, and administrators obtain relevant information while becoming effective users of the Internet.

AskERIC is sponsored by ERIC, the Educational Resources Information Center. A program of the U.S. Department of Education, ERIC is the world's largest source of information related to education. ERIC/IT, located at Syracuse University, is one of 16 clearinghouses carrying out the work of the ERIC system. It specializes in library/information science and educational technology, and it is committed to helping users benefit from the wealth of knowledge contained in ERIC. The Ask-ERIC Project is a reflection of this commitment.

The hallmark of AskERIC is the human intermediary, who interacts with the information seeker and personally selects and delivers information within 48 hours of receiving an inquiry. The benefit of the human-mediated service is that it allows AskERIC staff to determine the precise information needs of the client and to present an array of relevant resources, both from the ERIC system and from the vast resources of "The 'Net."

AskERIC began with service to three state networks, who made the service readily accessible to their users as a network menu option. In the months since its inception, AskERIC has expanded to additional state and regional networks. Recent increases in the number of users, and repeat users, suggest an ongoing need for this form of information service.

PURPOSE

Drawing on the full services of the ERIC system, AskERIC provides users with a wide range of education-related services through a single gateway:

- Answers to education questions
- Full text ERIC Digests and Help Sheets
- Training and reference materials for Internet use
- An intermediary between users and other ERIC subject-specialized clearinghouses
- Referrals to other appropriate education resources

- Referrals to appropriate network information sources, such as listservs, bulletin boards, and Gopher/FTP sites.

THE AskERIC ELECTRONIC LIBRARY

The AskERIC Electronic Library is a Gopher/FTP site of selected education resources, including ERIC Digests, lesson plans, network information guides, bibliographies, the archives of several education-related listservs (such as KIDSPHERE, K12ADMIN, and LM_NET) and more. Users tap into the Electronic Library on their own to browse through a large bank of education information, much of which is in full text.

AskERIC USERS

AskERIC receives questions from a wide range of users. School teachers, library media specialists, and administrators compose the largest user group. University professors, university and school students, and public librarians also send questions. Questions are welcomed even when they do not originate from one of the targeted state or regional networks.

TYPES OF QUESTIONS

AskERIC receives a wide variety of questions, including:

- Content specific (K-12 classroom focus)
- Library media focus
- Internet-related
- Educational management
- Services provided by AskERIC
- Reference materials/sources

The most common questions are developed into Infoguides and other resources for the AskERIC Electronic Library, assuring that users' interests are always represented by readily available resources.

PARTICIPATING NETWORKS

At present, state and/or regional networks offer AskERIC as a menu option in New York, Texas, Florida, Massachusetts, Ohio, Washington, and California. A number of other state and regional networks are preparing to implement AskERIC.

IMMEDIATE AND FUTURE PLANS

- Parents AskERIC, an Internet service designed for parents to ask questions dealing with their children (began on September 1, 1993).

- Cooperation with ACCESS ERIC (an outreach arm of the ERIC system) to extend AskERIC services to users of commercial networks such as America Online and CompuServe.

- The continuing development of the AskERIC Electronic Library.

- Assisting in the development of Gopher sites on the Internet and at the Research Labs and Centers sponsored by the Office of Educational Research and Improvement, U.S. Department of Education.

- The hiring of additional staff to meet the increased need for AskERIC and to allow growth to more state networks.

IN SUMMARY

AskERIC is a vital and growing force in the educational community. It uses modern technology to send its information via the Internet, while at the same time maintaining personal communication through the use of trained specialists to assist K-12 educators in their search for information.

We are excited about AskERIC's success to date and are eager to expand AskERIC question-answering to new K-12 audiences and to further develop services and resources. To discuss options, please contact:

Nancy Morgan or Richard Tkachuck
AskERIC Coordinators
askeric@ericir.syr.edu

Michael B. Eisenberg
Director, ERIC/IT
mike@ericir.syr.edu

ADDRESS

To contact the question answering service, send e-mail to askeric@ericir.syr.edu.

To use the AskERIC Electronic Library, Gopher to ericir.syr.edu.

4

CD-ROM and the School Library Media Center

ROXANNE BAXTER MENDRINOS

The virtual library combines the contents of the on-site collection, in both print and electronic form, with the concept of remote access through an electronic network to worldwide resources—both library and commercial—for delivery to one's computer or terminal. The virtual library breaks down the confines of the on-site library collection and opens the doors to information available locally, nationally, and worldwide. It can link a variety of resources such as CD-ROMs, videos, text files, worldwide library catalogs, and optical discs, and it can facilitate the use of electronic mail. Multimedia CD-ROM is one of the doors to the virtual library and is redefining learning by creating a world that combines text, graphics, animation, video, and sound to expand and deepen the student's knowledge and awareness.

This learning process is not a passive one. The student controls the learning experience. He or she is the navigator through the virtual library. It is an ability to think and reason that will guide him or her through crevices and over mountains to the information that will end the quest. Success depends on this ability to satisfy information needs. Active mental involvement, self-discovery, and learning by doing, all crucial elements in inductive thinking, are the navigational tools of the student. Learning is fluid rather than static. The student is the questioner, immersed in inquiry. The mind of the student grows through these experiences that provide a sense of importance, power, and connection. Such self-directed education results in retaining 90 percent of what is learned.

Compare this rich educational adventure with the classroom textbook. The textbook is linear and passive, whereas the virtual experience stretches the imagination. Three integral components are necessary for the virtual library to be effective:

- A computerized network that is fully functional
- Information in digital form that is content rich
- A knowledgeable user

This article will discuss these three components of the virtual library in conjunction with CD-ROM technology. It will relate these concepts to the results from my study on the applications of CD-ROM technology in secondary-school library media centers.

NETWORKING

"Networking is a simple idea: the sharing of resources among computer users. Rather than duplicate the resource or transport it, the resource is provided to a user who may be some distance away via connections between computers" (Tennant, et al. 1993). Telecommunication networks, composed of worldwide online utilities, local area networks (LANs), online information services, online library catalogs, online bibliographic utilities and services, and that offer electronic mail and file transfer capabilities, provide the user with one-stop shopping for a multitude of information resources. The Internet is a global network of computers that makes a multitude of resources available worldwide through one's personal computer.

Networking facilitates sharing resources among computers and communication between computer users regardless of distance. CD-ROM networks allow users to share CD-ROM databases through local area networks within the school, through wide area networks (WAN) with remote areas such as Europe or Asia, or through remote dial-in by using a personal computer and a modem. Simultaneous use of a popular CD-ROM database by multiple users and multiple CD-ROM discs accessed at the same time by many users expand the concept of the stand-alone workstation through interconnectivity. Multiplatform network connectivity, offering the ability to link Macintosh and IBM microcomputers with Unix operating systems, and CD-ROM servers enabling different machines and protocols to communicate with each other are at the crux of networking in the nineties.

Out of the 301 library media centers (LMCs) using CD-ROM technology in this study (Mendrinos 1992a), only 4.5 percent were networking their CD-ROM workstations. However, one-third (91) of the library media centers planned to be networked soon. There is a growing interest in networking as more CD-ROM laserdiscs become networkable and are utilized by more students and classes.

Several CD-ROM networking solutions include

- A stand-alone CD-ROM workstation with multiple CD-ROM drives

- A peer-to-peer network

- A dedicated CD-ROM server

- A networked Novell fileserver, which contains the CD-ROM drive and data from multiple optical discs

Stand-Alone Configuration

The latest multimedia CD-ROM discs with sound, video, color, and graphics necessitate a powerful CD-ROM workstation. A workstation is defined as a stand-alone unit or a networked computer that uses the shared resources of servers but does not provide shared resources to other computers.

Multiple drives on a CD-ROM workstation can hold several discs of the same database indexed through several years, or they can include several different CD-ROM databases, each accessed through the menu option on the screen display.

The following specifications are the minimum requirements for CD-ROM workstations to accommodate the multimedia technology:

- A fast microprocessor (examples include the IBM 386DX at 33MHz and the IBM 486DX at 25MHz); if the workstation will be used as a server, the IBM 486DX series with speeds from 25MHz to 66MHz is recommended

- At least 8 MB (megabytes) of RAM (Random Access Memory)

- A hard disk with at least 100 MB of memory

- Non-interlacing Super VGA (Video Graphics Array) card (interlacing creates a flickering effect at high resolutions that can be very distracting) with at least 1 MB of memory and a speed of 70 Hz or greater for a screen refresher

- A fast CD-ROM drive, with a minimum transfer rate of 300 kbs (kilobytes per second), a double-spin drive, multisession capabilities, and CD-ROM XA Compliant.

The use of color to highlight features in the latest CD-ROM products warrants the use of a color monitor that is compatible with the Super VGA card. CD-ROM drives can be internal, like most floppy and hard drives, or external.

Peer-to-Peer Network

A second CD-ROM networking solution is the peer-to-peer network. This type of CD-ROM network allows any workstation on the network to contribute its resources concurrently with the resources of other networked workstations, and any workstation can be accessed remotely. In the peer-to-peer network, a nondedicated server acts as both a server and a workstation.

Dedicated CD-ROM Server

A third option is the dedicated server network, which is a networked computer acting solely as a server with no workstation capability. The main purpose of the dedicated CD-ROM server is to serve users on the network. A single CD-ROM server can support as many as 28 CD-ROM optical discs. Some CD-ROM servers can support multiple users sharing discs concurrently.

Novell File Server

Another option that schools with limited budgets and limited network staff should consider is copying CD-ROM software and data to the Novell file server located on the network.

Some of the advantages include the following:

- A Novell server can simultaneously support DOS or Macintosh "virtual" CD-ROMs
- Hard disk access is up to 20 times faster than CD access
- Hard disk storage is half the cost of a CD-ROM server
- Only one CD-ROM is required for the entire network
- The additional gigabytes of memory that are needed for this option are the only expense. (Jorgensen 1993)

Jodi Breau of Maine's Nokomis High School Library Media Center has networked discipline-specific classrooms, such as those for science and English classes, for sharing the CD-ROM technology, first using the LANtastics peer-to-peer network. She states:

> The Nokomis Library Media Center has changed from an extra place for study hall students to an actively working research facility. The computers and the CD-ROM technology have made the difference. Our vision for the future includes a building expansion and a network station in every classroom in our building and ultimately, the other libraries throughout the school district. Not until everyone has equal access to the resources will this project be successful. (Mendrinos 1994)

Pat Cheek of Maryland's Queen's County High School shares her networking experiences:

> The Media Center was chosen as the site of the first network. First the library became the focal point for computer usage. Students and staff that previously did not utilize the center began to see ways the resources could enhance their teaching or studying. As administrators saw the increased demand for computer time, money was allocated for additional networks and the library budget was increased to allow revenue for additional software, namely computer databases. Secondly, the location of the network within the Media Center promoted the feeling that the computers could be scheduled by any class and no subject area had preference over another.
>
> Today the Media Center at the main building is one of five instructional networks. All networks, operating on a token ring interconnection, communicate with others and any patron using a computer can access software, including catalog information and CD-ROM databases, from any computer within the building. (Mendrinos 1994)

CD-ROM TECHNOLOGY

The second component of the virtual library is the importance of the content of the digitized electronic information. There are over 3,000 CD-ROM discs published, with the number increasing daily. The CD-ROM publishing challenge is to create richly informative yet visually and aurally spellbinding CD-ROM experiences.

The latest CD-ROM disc holds 300,000 pages of information, is over 700 megabytes, and includes full motion. Increased multimedia opportunities have been made possible by increased data transfer rates, increased rotational speeds, improved average access times, multisession capabilities, CD-ROM XA compression and interleaving, and special features such as digital audio over the SCSI interface (Sund 1993).

CD-ROM XA has made possible multimedia, multiplatform, and multilingual capabilities, expanding markets in business, education, and entertainment. It has made possible the proliferation of multimedia data exchange, the delivery of text, data graphics, audio, and video to end-users in a faster and better way. CD-ROM XA interleaves and compresses audio, video, and text data into a single file without using a lot of processing power. It creates the illusion of simultaneous sound and pictures, making the multimedia presentation more pleasing to the observer.

The term *multiplatform* designates one disc that is used in different computer platforms. Discs are available for any computer workstation. Multiplatform retrieval software allows the CD-ROM disc to be accessed by a variety of CD-ROM drives, hardware, and networking environments. Multilingual capabilities allow the CD-ROM disc to present the content in several languages, offering the user the option of interactively changing the start-up language of the disc.

Wireless technology, which has led to the implementation and success of paging systems and the cellular telephone, is being utilized in CD-ROM production. Sony has developed a hand-held, wireless, self-contained CD-ROM XA player combining pictures, graphics, audio, and moving images with a vast text storage all of which can be plugged into a television. It can be used with databases for educational use, or it can be taken on the job to provide instant access to information in CD-ROM manuals. Wireless technology is challenging business, education, and entertainment companies to rethink information delivery and publishing inside and outside the company, home, and educational institution.

Can library media specialists afford to ignore the virtual information explosion? *Newsweek* and *Time* magazines are producing interactive multimedia magazines on the CD-ROM optical disc. *Newsweek*'s premier issue, "Unfinished Business: Minding the Earth," includes authorities such as Jane Goodall and David Brower speaking about the earth, over 80 *Washington Post* articles on environmental topics from last year, computer animations on topics from the formation of acid rain to the destruction of the ozone layer, and narrated photo essays on green economics and air pollution, to mention just a few features. Imagine if this disc was networked to science, social studies, and English classes as well as the media center available through remote access.

An increasing number of textbooks are becoming interactive, seriously challenging the classroom to reduce its linear focus. The CD-ROM version of D. C. Heath's popular textbook *The Enduring Vision* includes the complete textbook searchable by keyword with video clips such as scenes of World War II, primary archival documents such as the Bill of Rights, as well as animated maps and charts. For example, an instructor can display a demographic map of the African American population in 1790 and through animation illustrate its growth over 200 years. Interactivity through multimedia access gives the text several dimensions, creating a living period of history enveloping the student. The ability to increase video response time on networks means that multimedia textbooks will be networked to the library media center as well as the classroom, and they will be made available to homes through remote access.

Multimedia encyclopedias such as the new *Grolier*, Microsoft *Encarta,* and *Compton's* expand literacy through the visual, auditory, tactile, and textual images of knowing. *Compton's Interactive Encyclopedia* bundles Ami Pro 3.0 for Windows, enabling information transfer directly to the word processor with article dictations automatically being added to the document. This encyclopedia provides a virtual workplace where many articles, pictures, and atlases can be created at one time and made available on the desktop. The increased number and quality of the graphics on the screen produce a significantly enhanced multimedia interactive encyclopedia. Normal speech recognition for retrieving articles is the next phase for this encyclopedia. The public library, community college and four-year college libraries, and the school district can network their CD-ROM resources and share the costs of increasing information access.

With Kodak's Photo CD capabilities, teachers can take their photographs, negatives, transparencies, flat art, and digital files of pictures on floppy disk to a photo CD store and have the images digitized for CD format. With the Kodak Shoebox Photo CD Image Manager software, teachers can organize their images for slide shows by automatically displaying their visuals through the computer. Teachers can have their Photo CDs available on the network for interactive use.

The *Animals* CD-ROM from the experts at the San Diego Zoo takes the child on an in-depth visual and auditory adventure into a colorful virtual reality that provides a wonderful knowledge-filled and insightful experience of the lives and habitats of 200 exotic animals. The *Clinton* CD-ROM and the *Desert Storm* CD-ROM bring recent periods of history to life through video, audio, maps, charts, and text. Multimedia challenges students to change and seek new directions in their thinking processes.

From my research, the most popular commercial discs were found to be encyclopedias, magazine indexes, and newspaper indexes. CD-ROM was the preferred format, over both online and print resources. Reasons included:

- CD-ROM provides unlimited access
- The need for library assistance is minimal
- CD-ROM is easier to use
- CD-ROM has predictable costs
- Students use the same searching and thinking strategies
- Students perform their own searches (Mendrinos 1992a)

Nearly twice as many library media specialists agreed that CD-ROM products are an improvement over print. Reasons included:

- Accessibility
- Immediate gratification
- Increased use by students
- Faster and easier to use
- Ease of obtaining printed results
- Excellent division of topics into subtopics
- More efficient space allocation

- Multiple access points

- Students preferred the CD-ROM disc over print when both were available

- Motivation and productivity increased for special-education students, learning-disabled students, and average students (Mendrinos 1992b)

CD-ROM does not eliminate print; it increases the use of print. Library media specialists who use CD-ROM have larger periodical and microfiche collections, and students are pointed in the direction of relevant print resources. One library media specialist stated:

> Students go to Infotrac or Newsbank. I keep track of the fiche that we are using. I have to evaluate the use of it. Unfortunately, it's getting expensive and we have to justify it. When I discuss cutting the CD-ROMs with students and teachers, they are all aghast—"Oh, you can't get rid of that, we use it too much!" (Mendrinos 1992a)

The most popular databases in Maine and Pennsylvania were the state-sponsored union catalogs, containing 2 and 12 million volumes respectively. Familiarity with and positive attitudes toward CD-ROM are fostered through the use of statewide databases, which leads to increased use of this technology. Library media specialists using the CD-ROM statewide union catalogs shared these thoughts:

> It's amazing! These two discs have all these holdings from 800 libraries. You can actually sit down and have all this information right at your fingertips. (Mendrinos 1992a)

> My students come back and share with me, "I've gotten an A on those papers. I don't think I would have if I didn't have the Access PA database to help me get all those books." In the case where the student has to read a book and can't get it anywhere, he or she is able to get the book through Access PA. One of my students exclaimed, "That really saved my life!" (Mendrinos 1992a)

In Maryland, according to Pat Cheek, the 11th-grade state pilot assessment test includes such tasks as writing editorials regarding the benefits or problems with a proposed nuclear plant, developing a proposal for a health and wellness course, a global warming mock trial, schools of the twenty-first century, and a fast food restaurant proposal. All work is collected and sent to state officials for grading. The results are synthesized and, ultimately, both the county and the individual school receive a report card (Mendrinos 1992a).

A major aspect of the assessment test is performing research. The test requires that specific time be set aside for library use. The technology in the media center is invaluable in allowing large numbers of students to search several databases simultaneously in a short span of time. The media center could not accommodate all the students wishing to use computers, so other networks were utilized. SIRS on CD-ROM, Infotrac's Magazine Index and Health and Science Index, as well as Newsbank's Index on CD-ROM were most valuable. Virtual access to information—the ability to access and retrieve information at any time, from anywhere, in order to solve an information need—was a necessity.

A KNOWLEDGEABLE USER

The third and the most important component of the virtual library is the user. Success is dependent on how the student navigates the virtual library to access, retrieve, gather, analyze, evaluate, and apply the information. Is the student information-literate? Does he or she have the critical-thinking abilities necessary for success?

According to the SCANS report prepared by the U.S. Department of Labor, every worker must have certain competencies with information in order to achieve world-class standards in a global economy. A worker must have the abilities to

- Acquire and evaluate information

- Organize and maintain information

- Interpret and communicate information

- Use computers to process information (1991)

Information literacy in a resource-learning environment fosters these competencies articulated by the U.S. Department of Labor.

According to one study on CD-ROM technology, the "at risk" learner *is* positively affected and encouraged to learn. The following effects were observed:

- Special-education students, learning-disabled students, and average students were more responsive to CD-ROM than to print indexes.

- CD-ROM was a great equalizer by helping students with learning disabilities and average abilities bridge their gap with high-ability students.

- CD-ROM expanded the students' thinking abilities.

- CD-ROM helped students to think in concise terms.

- Special-education students and staff had higher expectations.

- CD-ROM helped students to think in more concrete terms, which benefited the lower-level students.

Special-education students and staff had higher expectations when using the CD-ROM technology. Special-education and mainstreamed students used it by themselves, without assistance.

Electronic tools allow the user to map concepts and ideas, to outline terms visually as well as abstractly while being in control of the tactile manipulation of the data. This navigation through the data liberates the navigator from linear thinking. It promotes diverse thinking, branching, searching for connections, exploring and creating new constructs, and forming bridges to new knowledge paths. The mechanics of CD-ROM technology and network information retrieval, relative to the issues of hardware and software, are superficially easy. However, there are larger questions related to its use. For example, does the library media specialist form a bridge between the mechanical manipulation and the internal thinking and learning processes of the student?

The mechanical manipulation of the hardware and software alone can help the student work through the program. It is the thinking and learning processes within the student that need to be developed to guide him or her to make associations, to relate terms, to narrow topics, and to think in parallel ways to successfully access and retrieve information electronically. Without the development of these thought processes, electronic access and retrieval will be overwhelming for the student. The phenomenal growth of electronic text, journals, and databases available on the Internet is one example that requires these thinking processes for successful navigation and retrieval. This is a lifelong skill not only for the student but for the educator.

The goal of the school library media specialist should be to create self-sufficient users of the virtual library. Four major elements necessary for the successful user interface include:

1. In-service training

2. The use of formal classroom instruction

3. Development of an information curriculum

4. Making time for instruction.

In-Service Training

To become effective leaders in implementing the new technology, library media specialists should take continuing-education workshops or hire consultants to keep their skills state-of-the-art. If CD-ROM technology is to be used effectively, as a stand-alone unit or networked in a virtual library environment, then faculty training is critical. Faculty should know

• How to use the technology with confidence

• What is available on CD-ROM discs that relates to their particular discipline

• How to integrate CD-ROM technology into their classroom teaching

• How to incorporate critical thinking and the information literacy process into students' interaction with the technology

Of the 301 library media specialists using CD-ROM in my study, only 53 percent offered in-service training for faculty. There are significant direct relationships in the number of faculty trained and the level of use of CD-ROM technology in the respective curriculum areas. The more faculty that receive training in using CD-ROM, the higher the percentage of use within the curriculum area. Faculty awareness of CD-ROM increases student use of the technology within the discipline. The curriculum changes to reflect the additional resources and the currency of the available information.

One of the library media specialists reflected, "Science and English use CD-ROM databases more often. . . . There is a rush for more current up to date science material and the students like the fact that they can get more information without waiting for the book to be printed" (Mendrinos 1992). With the proliferation of consumer CD-ROM drives, library media specialists may expand their training to include the community.

Formal Classroom Instruction

Formal classroom instruction in CD-ROM technology within the virtual library and in the thinking strategies necessary to effectively apply the power of CD-ROM increased both its use within the particular disciplines of the faculty and its use by students to satisfy their personal goals and leisure interests. Opportunities for formal instruction in CD-ROM databases increased when more faculty received training.

Different types of training can help students and faculty broaden their critical-thinking strategies, expand or narrow their thesis statements, and develop lifelong learning skills in analysis and information access and retrieval that can relate to success in navigating the virtual library. Library media specialists need to increase both faculty and administration training and formal classroom instruction, as well as expand the period of time for instructing new users so that they might learn more than just the mechanics of the software and hardware.

Development of an Information Curriculum

Another interesting finding is that school board approval of the library's curriculum increases faculty in-service and formal classroom instruction in the use of CD-ROM. Significant direct relationships were found especially between school board approval and the number of science faculty being trained. Does your information science curriculum need to be created or updated to include the concepts of the virtual library?

Making Time for Instruction

The use of CD-ROM technology as a good tool for teaching critical thinking was mentioned by all the library media specialists interviewed. Classes that made time for CD-ROM instruction, in periods of 45 minutes to two hours, showed increased use of the CD-ROM technology and an increased transfer of learning from academic to personal use. The more classes trained in CD-ROM, the higher level of use in the specific discipline. Longer instructional periods sharpen the intellect, promoting the thinking processes and analytical abilities of the students. The type and length of instruction offered has significant consequences for the self-sufficient searcher's ability to effectively use CD-ROM technology.

Charmaine Gates of Archbishop Carroll High School in Radnor, Pennsylvania, shares her experience:

> The list the teacher handed me had most of the things you associate with moral issues: abortion, drug and alcohol abuse, child abuse, sexual abuse, rape, pornography, drug control, free speech, etc. With these general topics, and working with small groups of four and five at the computer, my assistant and I were able to teach these groups the following:

- How to use the CD-ROM laserdisc to narrow the topic before they started

- What they had to know about a subject before they decided on a viewpoint

- How much information they really did need to give a fifteen minute presentation

- How to distinguish which sources would give them the most information

Due to the informal nature of this tutorial work, measures of the outcome would naturally be the project. The teacher was certainly impressed by the results. It was also interesting to see that when, a few weeks later, a science teacher happened to assign a "small extra credit assignment" on the ecological current events to those who had been in these classes, these students approached the computer and made competent decisions without the "nursemaiding" of the library staff that they had needed only weeks before. (Mendrinos 1994)

FUNDING

Library media specialists stressed the importance of utilizing public relations and defining educational needs that would lead to increased administrative support. The cooperation of the administration enables library media centers to have access to funding from the local school district, as well as special federal funds such as Chapter II.

Several library media specialists expressed their thoughts. One said, "It's not the student enrollment that correlates with increases in CD-ROM use or the need for more workstations, it is the educational need that determines an increase in the use of CD-ROM technology and the demand for more workstations" (Mendrinos 1992a). Another said, "I tend to feel I have a lot of support but I tend to do a lot of public relations" (Mendrinos 1992a).

Pat Cheek shares her strategy:

In order to keep up the monetary momentum I continually plug computer-based research among the staff. When I know a class is going to be using computers for this purpose, I invite my principal, supervisor, etc., to come in and watch the students. As they say, "A picture is worth a thousand words, memos, etc." They are so impressed with the enthusiasm of the students and the hands-on activity, that the program sells itself. Of course, it doesn't hurt that the local newspapers have written articles on our computer networks, that TV shows have been produced featuring our school's computer setup and that visitors as far away as Chile, England and Australia have come to view our technology. (Mendrinos 1994)

CD-ROM promotes increased circulation and the increased use of the library media center. CD-ROM is changing the stereotypical images of the library media specialist and the library media center into images that are more positive and trend setting. A strong majority (90 percent) of the library media specialists surveyed believe that the technology has had a positive effect on how their faculty and students perceive them.

Multimedia CD-ROM and the virtual library are creating new worlds for the information search. Be part of this navigational challenge and prepare your students and your faculty for this adventure. Examine your library media center and plan, implement, and evaluate ways of networking your resources and your school community to the world. Create partnerships with the computer staff, faculty, and administrators to make the information journey a reality.

REFERENCES

Jorgensen, Gilbert. 1993. Dynix CD-ROM Networking Worksheets. Provo, UT: Dynix Scholar Networking.

Mendrinos, Roxanne. 1994. *Building Information Literacy: A Guide to Schools and Libraries.* Englewood, CO: Libraries Unlimited.

———. 1992a. "Applications of CD-ROM Technology for Reference Purposes: A Survey of Secondary School Library Media Specialists in Pennsylvania and Maine." *Dissertation Abstracts International* (University Microfilms 9217458).

———. 1992b. "CD-ROM and At-Risk Students: A Path to Excellence." *School Library Journal* (October): 29-31.

Sund, Alan. 1993. "Maintaining Continuity in CD-ROM Development." *CD-ROM Professional* (January): 8.

Tennant, Roy, John Ober, and Anne G. Lipow. 1993. *Crossing the Internet Threshold: An Instructional Handbook.* Berkeley, CA: Library Solutions Press.

What Work Requires of Schools: A SCANS Report for America 2000. 1991. Secretary's Commission on Achieving Necessary Skills. Washington, DC: U.S. Department of Labor.

5

Distance Education
The Virtual Classroom Updated

DANIEL D. BARRON

This entry provides background that builds on the article "Distance Education and School Library Media Specialists" in *School Library Media Annual 1991*, vol. 9, and lists resources to develop information service programs for teachers and students. Both historical background and support for continued in-house education are included in the resource list.

DISTANCE EDUCATION: WHAT DOES IT MEAN?

Distance education takes advantage of currently available technologies to achieve two objectives of teaching and learning: 1) Providing equitable access to quality education, and 2) meeting the unique learning needs and styles of individuals.

Educators began experimenting with radio in the early twenties, television in the early thirties, and computers in the early fifties because they anticipated the importance of these media to students in K-12 schools. Today, sophisticated information and educational delivery systems are in place and there is the promise of even more responsive systems becoming available in the near future to support teachers and students.

School library media specialists can play an important leadership role in helping teachers not only to accommodate this inevitable addition to their schools, but also to enjoy integrating it successfully into their classes. For a rationale and process for doing this, the contemporary school library media specialist need not go very far beyond the guidelines already promulgated for the profession in *Information Power: Guidelines for School Library Media Programs*. Distance education, when viewed as an extension of the technology uses suggested in *Information Power,* demands basically the same roles already outlined—working in partnership with the subject specialist teacher, providing information services to support students and teachers, helping students and teachers to use the full range of available information and educational technologies, and managing the systems and processes for equitable access.

Distance education has its roots in the area of correspondence study and can be considered to be an evolutionary step in extending educational opportunity to the geographically remote, physically challenged, or otherwise place-bound person. In addition to providing a much wider range of options for these groups, current applications of distance education afford a richer variety of opportunities for those not so challenged or remote. Both the effectiveness and the importance of using distance education depend to a great extent upon the definitions of *educational opportunities* and whether or not teachers have the capability and willingness to implement the technology into their teaching and professional decision making.

DISTANCE EDUCATION: CONCEPTS AND DEFINITIONS

There are a wide variety of words and phrases that are often used interchangeably in this area of education. Though it may not necessarily be essential to standardize the vocabulary, there are sufficient illustrations in the literature to warrant a more common reference language.

distance education—The holistic consideration of all aspects of this subfield of education including the knowledge base, ongoing research, initial and continuing education in the field, integration of other disciplines, evaluation, delivery systems and technologies, and all other elements necessary to successfully implement and perpetuate teaching and learning.

long-distance education—The delivery of instruction and student learning over telecommunication networks. A carry-over from telephone services, but not necessary in the educator's vocabulary.

short-distance education—The delivery of instruction and student learning within the school building, the school district, or a substate region.

distance learning—The process of learning, for the student within distance education—the goal of distance education.

distance teaching—The process of teaching, for the teacher within distance education. This includes instructional design, presentation, interaction with students, follow-up activities such as testing and mentoring, and other instructional activities.

DISTANCE EDUCATION VIA TELEVISION

Perhaps a comparison of the generally accepted definitions for *instructional television* and *educational television* can help sort out the various uses of television in the classroom. Instructional television has generally been the term reserved for programming that has been specifically developed and scripted with learner outcomes in mind, and that is generally aired during regular school hours during the day. Educational television is usually defined as any programming that serves more than just a recreational function, and is often used in reference to the programming included on public television.

Whereas educational television is expected to inform and raise awareness, instructional television is designed to assure learning. Instructional television has made use of airplanes flying over a defined geographic region, closed-circuit statewide systems, Instructional Television Fixed Services (ITFS), and satellite delivery.

One of the most dramatic and widely known programs to incorporate the use of instructional television is the Star Schools Project that began with federal funding in the late eighties. Today, all the initial projects are still in operation, providing a wide range of live, interactive, distance-learning opportunities. Evaluations of these projects have been very positive. Based on this success, a wide range of other providers have begun similar services.

The television industry, including cable television, has responded to the frequent reference to television programming as the "vast wasteland of the intellect" or the "couch potato's domain." In developing what some have labeled "infotainment television," the industry has created a tremendously wide range of programming that, on the surface at least, represents an effort to help expand the knowledge base of viewers while it entertains them. The recent controversy involving Whittle's Channel One project has stimulated the more traditional program and service providers to mount and provide their own "services" to the school systems of the nation. Cable in the Classroom is one such effort and has provided subscription-free cable connections to thousands of schools throughout the nation.

Infotainment television can include the raft of cooking shows, nature programs, documentaries, and information specials that are aired on public television, cable channels, and commercial network television. Creative teachers can use much of this type of programming in the classroom, but only if they know what programs are available and what programs have instructional potential. The library media specialist can play a critical role in educating teachers as to the potential as well as providing the intellectual access to the schedules and ancillary materials that often accompany such programming. An important concept that teachers must believe and practice is that television, like all other technology, must be integrated into curricula, courses, classes, and assignments. If television, or any other application of technology, including the media program itself, is viewed as "support" or "enrichment," educators concerned with perpetuating innovation in these areas are out of luck.

It is both disturbing and amusing to hear people talk about "books and other media" or continue to argue over the definition of "educational" technology. Any technology that is used for educational purposes qualifies as educational technology (e.g., cars in driver's education, ranges in home economics, power saws in shop). No one medium can be expected to satisfy all the information needs, learning styles, presentation objectives, or human learning needs that exist in the school. However true this may be, and however often there is admonishment to go beyond the textbook and lecture to accomplish learning, the cloud of ignorance that tradition and unenlightened experience create among many teachers, administrators, parents, and students remains to be faced.

Television is often associated with the negative issues mentioned, and it is often considered merely an entertainment medium. Both teachers and library media specialists may have to do some reeducating of parents, the community, administrators, and even students. Parents and the community can be a strong support group for adding additional television sets, videocassette recorders, or cabling. However, parents and the community can be a tremendous stumbling block if their ideas about television are not expanded beyond the traditional and generally accepted definitions and associations.

Administrators are often overlooked among those attempting innovations in the classroom and media center. The expanded use of television carries with it a price tag, the same as any innovation. The administrator of the school is the key person to help obtain the resources to implement and expand any innovation. Most of them are not as educated in the use of technology as media specialists or teachers, yet they are required to help develop budgets to support the programs of both. Administrators also are responsible for job performance evaluation, and they require enough information to do that well. The latter is especially critical with innovative approaches to teaching and learning, for which the administrator has no academic or experiential preparation.

BEYOND TELEVISION

Distance education is often associated with television and satellite communications, but as the history of technology use by the profession would predict, distance educators are taking advantage of all current and developing technologies to provide distance education. The development of the Internet, often called the information superhighway, has an encompassing role to play with the promises of direct desktop-to-desktop audio and video links, an ever-expanding number of sites for accessing information and resources, and the potential of linking students and teachers in global discussions and conversations. As Integrated Services Digital Networks (ISDNs) become almost as accessible on local carriers as simple telephone connections, teachers and students will be able to share a virtual classroom, a virtual hallway, a virtual student center, a virtual library—a virtual campus. What can be said regarding the effective integration of television can also be said regarding the use of the Internet and other telecommunications technologies.

CONCLUSIONS

Distance education provides immediate access to information and instruction that can be integrated into existing classes and courses. It also provides opportunities to access classes and courses not otherwise available to the local school. In addition, it provides a model for all of education, and its implementation into existing curricula can upgrade those curricula.

The admonishments to teachers to take students beyond the textbook and lecture, to get them actively involved in the learning process, to engage them in collaborative learning experiences, to give them the tools for a lifelong process of continued education, to help them to effectively assimilate the use of available and developing technologies into their learning and decision making, and to provide them with opportunities to recognize their existence in and dependence on a global society are all arguments for making use of distance education in its many and varied forms.

The role of the library media specialist in distance education, though greatly expanded by the knowledge required and the new activities to manage, remains basically the same as it is stated in *Information Power*: "to help students and staff to become effective users of ideas and information."[1]

DISTANCE EDUCATION AND TELECOMMUNICATIONS RESOURCES FOR SCHOOL LIBRARY MEDIA SPECIALISTS

Background and Rationale for the Information Society

Brand, Stewart. 1988. *The Media Lab: Inventing the Future at MIT*. New York: Penguin.

Breivik, Patricia, and E. Gordon Gee. 1989. *Information Literacy: Revolution in the Library*. New York: Macmillan.

Papert, Seymour. 1993. *The Children's Machine*. New York: Basic Books.

Perelman, Lewis. 1993. *School's Out: Hyperlearning, the New Technology, and the End of Education*. New York: Morrow.

Rheingold, Howard. 1993. *The Virtual Community: Homesteading on the Electronic Frontier*. New York: Addison-Wesley.

Roszak, Theodore. 1986. *The Cult of Information: The Folklore of Computers and the True Art of Thinking*. New York: Pantheon.

Tehranian, Majid. 1990. *Technologies of Power: Information Machines and Democratic Prospects*. Norwood, NJ: Ablex.

Toffler, Alvin. 1990. *Power Shift: Knowledge, Wealth, and Violence at the Edge of the 21st Century*. New York: Bantam Books.

White, Mary Alice. 1987. *What Curriculum for the Information Age?* Hillsdale, NJ: Lawrence Erlbaum.

Wurman, Richard Saul. 1989. *Information Anxiety*. New York: Doubleday.

History, Background, Philosophy, and Guides

Barron, Daniel. 1989. "Distance Education: Removing Barriers to Knowledge." *School Library Journal*, vol. 35, no. 15: 28-33.

———. 1991. "E-Mail: Linking Schools in the Net." *Online Searcher*, vol. 3, no. 2: 1-23.

———. 1989. "The School Library Media Specialist and Distance Education." *School Library Media Activities Monthly*, vol. 5, no. 6: 49-50.

———. 1989. "Television: Our Forgotten Medium, Part I." *School Library Media Activities Monthly*, vol. 6, no. 4: 49-51.

———. 1990. "Television: Our Forgotten Medium, Part II." *School Library Media Activities Monthly*, vol. 6, no. 5: 47-49.

Bond, Sally. 1989. *Telecommunications-Based Distance Learning: A Guide for Local Educators.* Southeastern Educational Improvement Laboratory. P.O. Box 12746, 200 Park Offices, Suite 204, Research Triangle Park, NC 27709 (919) 549-8216.

Brown, James, Richard Lewis, and Fred Harcleroad. 1969. *AV Instruction: Media and Methods.* New York: McGraw-Hill.

Burke, Michael. 1989. *Distance Education and the Changing Role of the Library Media Specialist.* Syracuse University: ERIC Clearinghouse on Information Resources, Document IR-85.

Cyrs, Thomas, and Frank Smith. 1990. *Teleclass Teaching: A Resource Guide.* 2d ed. Las Cruces, NM: New Mexico State University.

Darrow, Ben H. 1932. *Radio: The Assistant Teacher.* Columbus, OH: R. G. Adams.

Diamond, Robert M. 1964. *A Guide to Instructional Television.* New York: McGraw-Hill.

From Linking to Learning and *Bridges to Learning*. A project of Annenberg/CPB, these two 30-minute videos provide excellent introductions to the use of distance education and converging technologies. Each is $29 for half-inch or $45 for three-quarter-inch video tape. For additional information call (800) LEARNER.

Going the Distance: A Handbook for Developing Distance Degree Programs Using Television Courses and Telecommunications Technologies. 1992. Prepared by Toby Levine Communications, Inc., Bethesda, MD: Annenberg/CPB and the PBS Adult Learning Service.

Jones, Maxine. 1985. *See, Hear, Interact: Beginning Developments in Two-Way Television.* Metuchen, NJ: Scarecrow Press.

Kurtz, E. B. 1959. *Pioneering in Educational Television: 1932-1939.* University of Iowa.

Lamb, Brian. *C-Span: America's Town Hall.* Acropolis Books, 1988. An excellent resource that describes the development and impact of the C-Span access to political and other social affairs.

Moore, Michael, et al. 1990. *The Effects of Distance Learning: A Summary of Literature.* University Park, PA: American Center for the Study of Distance Education, Penn State University (403 S. Allen St., Suite 206, State College, PA 16801-5202).

Ostendorf, Virginia. 1989. *What Every Principal, Teacher and School Board Member Should Know About Distance Education.* Littleton, CO: Virginia Ostendorf.

Journals and Periodicals

The American Journal of Distance Education. American Center for the Study of Distance Education. College of Education, Rackley Building, The Pennsylvania State University, University Park, PA 16802.

Distance Education and Technology Newsletter. Joan E. Connick, Distance Education Publications, RFD #2, Box 7290, #3, Winthrop, ME 04364 (207) 395-4615 (monthly, $40/year).

Education Satlink. 2100 I-70 Dr. Southwest, Columbia, MO 65203-4685 (800) 243-3376 (monthly, $90). The essential guide to education opportunities and schedules from satellite broadcast. If your school has a satellite dish, this resource is a must purchase.

Electronic Learning. Scholastic Inc., 555 Broadway, New York, NY 10012 (212) 505-4900 (8 issues, $24/year).

Information Searcher: A Newsletter for Teaching Online/CD-ROM Searching in Education. Datasearch Group Inc., 14 Hadden, Scarsdale, NY 10583 or call (914) 723-3156 (quarterly, $34).

Internet Research: Electronic Networking Applications and Policy. Mecklermedia Corporation, 11 Ferry Lane West, Westport, CT 06880 (203) 226-6967 (quarterly, $39/year).

Internet World. Mecklermedia Corporation, 11 Ferry Lane West, Westport, CT 06880 (203) 226-6967 (monthly, $29/year individuals; $59/year institutions).

Online Access. 900 N. Franklin, Suite 310, Chicago, IL 60610 (312) 573-1700 (monthly, $30).

Satellite Orbit. CommTek Publishing, 8330 Boone Blvd., Suite 600, Vienna, VA 22180 (800) 792-5541. This is the most comprehensive resource available for all programming available via satellite.

T.H.E. (Technological Horizons in Education) Journal. 150 El Camino Real, Suite 112, Tustin, CA 92680-3670. Fax: (714) 730-3739 (monthly, free).

Technology and Learning. 330 Progress Rd., Dayton, OH 45449 (monthly, $24/year).

Technos: Quarterly for Educators for Education and Technology. Agency for Instructional Technology, Box A, Bloomington, IN 47402 (812) 339-2203 (quarterly, $20/year).

Cable and Satellite Resources

For the most complete listing of non-network programs and services see *Education Satlink* (listed above), "The Clearinghouse."

A&E
Arts & Entertainment, 555 Fifth Ave., New York, NY 10017. Contact Carole Kealy, Director of Community Development. (Special project with ALA, "The A&E Library Theater . . . Where Great Ideas Come to Life.")

ASTS
Arts and Sciences Teleconference Service, Oklahoma State University, 206 Life Science East, Stillwater, OK 74078 (405) 624-5647. Ask for information about their satellite network and to be put on their mailing list for *Learning by Satellite Newslink.*

BET
Black Entertainment Television, 1212 New York Ave. NW, Suite 430, Washington, DC 20001 (703) 875-0430.

C-Span
"C-Span in the Classroom," C-Span, P.O. Box 75298, Washington, DC 20013 or call (800) 523-7586.

Cable in the Classroom (formerly Cable Alliance for Education), Bobbi Kamil, Executive Director, 1900 N. Beauregard St., Suite 108, Alexandria, VA 22311. Fax: (903) 845-1409.

CNN (News Access)
Connie Singleton, National School Boards Association, 1680 Duke St., Alexandria, VA 22314 (703) 838-6764.

CNN (Newsroom)
Ann Skinner, Educational Systems Corporation, c/o Media Management Services, Inc., 10 N. Main St., Yardley, PA 19067-9986 or call (800) 344-6219.

Channel One, The Classroom Channel, and The Educators' Channel
Whittle Communications, 505 Market St., Knoxville, TN 37902 or call (615) 595-5100.

The Discovery Channel (Assignment Discovery)
The Discovery Channel, Box AD, 8201 Corporate Dr., Landover, MD 20785 or call (800) 321-1832. Ask specifically for information about the "Assignment Discovery Educator's Kit."

The Learning Channel (The Electronic Library)
Molly Breeden, Assistant Director of Educational Services, The Learning Channel, 1525 Wilson Blvd., Suite 550, Rosslyn, VA 22209 or call (800) 346-0032.

The Mind Extension University (The Education Network)
Don Sutton, Executive Director, The Mind Extension University, 9697 E. Mineral Ave., Englewood, CO 80112 or call (800) 525-7002.

The National Technological University
601 S. Howes, P.O. Box 700, Fort Collins, CO 80522 (303) 484-6050.

National University Teleconference Network (NUTN)
332 Student Union, Oklahoma State University, Stillwater, OK 74078 (405) 624-5191. A service for developing and promoting teleconferences, this group provides good information for faculty development as well as teleconferences that will be of interest to some students.

PBS Adult Learning Service
1320 Braddock Place, Alexandria, VA 22314-1698 or call (800) ALA-ALS8.

Star Schools
Technology Application Team, U.S. Department of Education. (202) 219-2267.

TWC
The Weather Channel, ABMS, 5020 McNeel Industrial Way, Powder Springs, GA 30073 (404) 801-2503.

Centers and Support

American Center for the Study of Distance Education, Penn State University, 403 S. Allen St., Suite 206, State College, PA 16801-5202.

The Annenberg/PBS Project, 901 E St. NW, Washington, DC 20004-2006.

Institute for the Transfer of Technology to Education, National School Boards Association, 1680 Duke St., Alexandria, VA 22314 or call (703) 838-6722.

The International Centre for Distance Learning at the UK Open University has a database open for free access. Telnet to acsvax.open.ac.uk At the welcome message please login to the Open University VAX cluster with the Username: **icdl.** We would then like you to access the database using your country name as Account code. Please enter this without any spaces. The Password is then just **AAA.** If you have any difficulty or want to comment, please send e-mail to n.ismail@open.ac.uk or l.r.a.melton@open.ac.uk. The Open University can also be reached via: Janet number 000041500030, EuropaNET 204334504891, Geonet da 23428440015630 or OU-VAX.

Library and Information Science Distance Education Consortium (LISDEC), Dan Barron, Coordinator, College of Library and Information Science, University of South Carolina, Columbia, SC 29208 or call (803) 777-4825, fax: (803) 777-7938 or BITNET: N400005@UNIVSCVM INTERNET:N400005@UNIVSCVM.CSD.SCAROLINA.EDU

The National Distance Learning Center: Owensboro Community College, 4800 New Hartford Rd., Owensboro, KY 42303 or call (502) 686-4558.

Other Related Resources

Directories

New Technology Consultants. *Satellite Programming Directory.* A directory of agencies and institutions that provide satellite-based telecommunications programming that includes the name and address of a contact person, the technical data necessary to receive the programming, and the scope of the programming. Available for $65 from NTC, P.O. Box 27044, Minneapolis, MN 55427.

1993-1994 Uplink & Downlink Directories. 7th ed. (2 vols.) Virginia Ostendorf, P.O. Box 2896, Littleton, CO 80161-2896 (303) 797-3131.

Computer-Based Distance Education

Children's Television Workshop
One Lincoln Plaza, New York, NY 10023 or call them at (212) 595-3456 to get information on their 3-2-1 Contact Database. They are providing a software package to help teachers use the award winning television series focusing on science and technology for 8 to 12 year olds.

Computer Pals
4974 SW Galen, Lake Oswego, OR 97035

Connected Education Inc.
92 Van Cortland Park South, No. 6F, Bronx, NY 10463 (212) 548-0435.

Electronic University Network
1150 Sansome St., San Francisco, CA 94111 (415) 956-7177.

SchoolLink
"To explore integrated curricular activities in science and social studies: to host discussions on topics of global interest, and to foster awareness among diverse student populations."
Contact Radio Shack Education Division (817) 390-2967.

E-Mail Utilities and Networks

For the most complete guide to state-level networks contact the Consortium for School Networking (CoSN), P.O. Box 65193, Washington, DC 20035 (202) 466-6296.

America Online (AOL), 8619 Westwood Center Dr., Vienna, VA 22182-9806.

AT&T Learning Network, P.O. Box 4012, Bridgewater, NJ 08807-4012 (800) 367-7225 or in Canada (800) 387-6100.

Classmate, DIALOG Information Services, Inc., 3460 Hillview Ave., Polo Alto, CA 94304 (800) 334-2564. Includes database searching in the DIALOG system as well as e-mail and some conferencing capabilities.

CompuServe, 500 Arlington Center Blvd., P.O. Box 20212, Columbus, OH 43220 (800) 848-8199.

Delphi, 3 Blackstone St., Cambridge, MA 02139 (800) 544-4005; in state (617) 491-3393.

FrEdMail Foundation, Box 243, Bonita, CA 92002-0243 (619) 475-4852.

GEnie, Box 02B-C, 401 N. Washington St., Rockville, MD 20850 (800) 638-9636.

Global Lab, Technical Education Research Center, Inc. (TERC), 2067 Massachusetts Ave., Cambridge, MA 02140 (617) 547-0430.

GTE Education Services (WorldClassroom), 8505 Freeport Pkwy., Suite 600, Irving, TX 75063 (800) 634-5644.

Iris On-Line Network, P.O. Box 42588, Washington, DC 20015-0588 (202) 298-0969.

Kids Network, National Geographic Society, 17th and M Sts., Washington, DC 20036 (800) 368-2728.

Learning Link, 1790 Broadway, 16th Floor, New York, NY 10019 (708) 390-8700.

MIX, EMS/McGraw-Hill, 9855 W. 78th St., Eden Prairie, MN 55344 (800) 622-6310.

Prodigy, 445 Hamilton Ave., White Plains, NY 10601 (914) 993-8000.

Unison Telecommunications Service, 700 W. Pete Rose Way, Cincinnati, OH 45203 (513) 723-1700.

X•Press X•Change, P.O. Box 4153, Englewood, CO 80155 (800) 772-6397. A news service which includes foreign presses (translated into English, but also available in French and Spanish).

Educational Resources Information Center (ERIC)

Access Eric, 1600 Research Blvd., Rockville, MD 20850 (800) 538-3742.

AskERIC, 800/LET ERIC or askeric@ericir.syr.edu.

ERIC for Teachers in Training: An Instructional Package for Professors that has been prepared by the staff of the ERIC Clearinghouse of Rural Education and Small Schools (P.O. Box 1348, Charleston, WV 25325).

Other Resources

Hunter, Beverly, and Erica Lodish. 1989. *Online Searching in the Curriculum: A Teaching Guide for Library Media Specialists and Teachers.* Denver, CO: ABC-CLIO.

Telecommunications: Concepts and Applications
5101 Madison Rd.
Cincinnati, OH 45227
(800) 543-7972
An excellent educational package to help you or your teachers learn about and use telecommunications technologies. Written specifically for use with students in elementary and secondary schools.

VideoPals
630 N. Tustin, Suite 165
Orange, CA 92667
(800) VID-PALS
Related to international sharing, kids can get the names and addresses of other schools to share videotapes of each other. Not e-mail, but another example of converging technologies in the Global Village.

Department of Education Online Service

The USDOE now provides toll-free access to an electronic bulletin board and data files that you and your school could find useful. You can register on your first dial in, but it takes a day or two for them to confirm that you are in fact an educator, the only requirement for the free service. The time you have is limited per call in, but you will find some interesting files and services available. One problem reported is that the line is frequently busy, especially during school hours. Using whatever modem and software you have, set it to no parity, eight data bits and one stop bit then dial (800) 222-4922. A menu will direct your responses.

NOTE

1. American Association of School Librarians, *Information Power: Guidelines for School Library Media Programs* (Chicago: American Library Association, 1988): 1.

Part II

Learning in the
Electronic Information Age

6

Thinking Skills for the Electronic Information Age

Applying Mental Capacity

ᛏ   **MARK VON WODTKE**   ᛐ

THE CHALLENGE

Information highways are emerging, but relatively few people know how to navigate and find what is there. By just moving their fingers, people can gather a great deal of information, but they typically do little synthesis. There are opportunities to set up virtual libraries, classrooms, and offices, but too few people know how to use this information environment for collaborative learning and working.

Simply put, a weak link in using the emerging computer applications and information infrastructure is *mental* capacity, not just computer capacity. McGraw-Hill has published a book I have written to address this problem. The book, *Mind over Media: Creative Thinking Skills for Electronic Media*, helps people learn how to work more effectively with the new information environment. There are three parts to *Mind over Media*:

PART I: THINKING
> provides a foundation in visual thinking and creative thought processes.

PART II: INTERACTING
> provides approaches for using electronic media more interactively.

PART III: MASTERING
> enhances ways anyone can get the most from his or her mind when using electronic media.

This book helps people learn universal thinking skills to enhance their mental capacity. If we can succeed at this, I believe a new renaissance could emerge, as in the past when cultures have assimilated new media. Let me draw from this book[1] and share with you ways to teach important thinking skills for the electronic information age.

MIND OVER MEDIA

People can learn more than which buttons to push. They can learn to work interactively using electronic media.

To work effectively with any tool requires more than simply having the tool. You must have the skill or technique to use the tool. You also need strategies or methods for working with it. In addition, you need a goal or objective that provides a positive mental attitude to open your mind to the possibilities the tool affords. Lacking any of these limits the benefit of the tool. As a result, the tool can even be a source of frustration.

Transportation involves using tools to move people and goods. For example, you are familiar with how to use an automobile for transportation. To get anywhere, you need a good vehicle, but you also need to be able to drive (or have a driver). In addition, you need a mental image or map of where you are going. And, of course, you need a destination and the ability to navigate. Although you usually don't consciously think about it, you need to address all of these levels to be able to use an automobile effectively.

Fig. 6.1. Generic levels.   **Fig. 6.2. Vehicular transportation.**

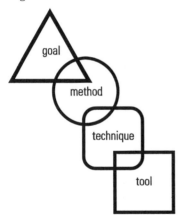 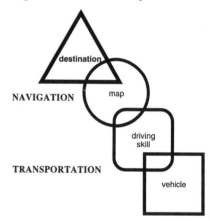

Communication involves moving ideas and information. Consider how you can relate your mind to media when using computers for communication. To be able to access electronic media, you need a good computer, but you also need to be able to use it (or have a computer operator). In addition, you need a mental model of where you are going. And, of course, you need an objective and the ability to find your way in what you are doing. As you can see, this involves both mind and media. You need to know more than how to just access the media—as you would just turning on a television. To work interactively with media using computers, you need to develop your mind, learning thinking skills that will help you navigate.

Fig. 6.3. Mind over media.

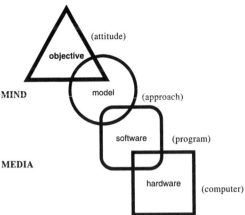

Different media are more effective in certain circumstances. Just as it is important to have access to multimodal transportation systems, it is also important to have access to multimedia communication systems. In some situations it makes sense to talk on the phone, or to write a handwritten note, or to make sketches you can FAX. Using telecommunications, you can access databases, move documents, or even interact with video. Both transportation and communication can give you a sense of freedom. With transportation you have the potential to go places and move goods. With communication you have the chance to explore ideas and transfer information.

NAVIGATING

People can learn to navigate in information environments.

Media space is an important notion that enables you to develop a sense of place when working with electronic media. Researchers in the System Concepts Laboratory at Xerox PARC coined the term *media space* in about 1985. Two of the researchers, Bob Stults and Steve Harrison, began to work in media space, using video as a design medium. They were looking for ways to extend physical space electronically. Their primary concern was the way in which the environment of electronic media interacts with the environment of physical space. They used video as an extension of their work setting for design and other collaborative endeavors. Their media space dealt with "the connection of real and imaginary places and the people and objects within them." They conducted several design projects using media space in this way.

By accessing electronic media using video and computers you can, in effect, create and experience new environments. William Gibson, a science fiction writer, refers to these environments as *Cyberspace*. Michael Sorkin writes about the *Electronic City* and its implications for society. Jaron Lanier coined the term *virtual reality* referring to environments you can enter and experience electronically. Many people are intrigued by creating artificial realities electronically.

Fig. 6.4. Map of media space—Cal Poly, Pomona.

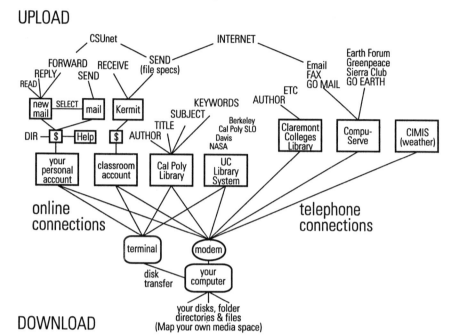

MAPPING MEDIA SPACE

People can develop cognitive maps of media space—the information environment they are working in.

In his book *Image of the City*, Kevin Lynch observed that people develop a mental image of a city. They identify nodes, paths, edges, and focal points to develop a sense of place so they can navigate. Cities with identifiable images are more accessible. The maps people draw of their image of a city depend upon what they understand and have access to. Children might just know the area around where they live. A taxi driver knows the districts of a city and the routes to get there. You use these images to develop a sense of place, not only in cities, but also work environments such as offices and schools. You have a mental image of where you put things in your file cabinet, desk, briefcase, and notebook.

Similarly, when working with electronic media, you need to develop a sense of place. You can do this by creating a clear image of the media space you work with. For example, you can make a branching diagram showing *directories* (folders) and *subdirectories* where you place files. Or you can diagram nodes you have access to and identify the paths you use to get there. These *cognitive maps* will help you develop a mental picture of where you are, what you can access, and how you can get there. This helps you remember where you put computer files; it also helps others find them. You can even diagram the frames of references you use in different application programs. This helps you access information when working in those programs. Identify what focal points (such as menus, icons, or markers) help you navigate. By working with familiar metaphors such as desktops, mailboxes, and classrooms you can quickly begin to develop a sense of place in the media space you use. Your media space will expand as you learn to use new applications and reach other computer environments through telecommunications. If you can clearly map your media space, then you can work more successfully with computers. With that comes a sense of confidence. Your whole attitude toward using electronic media can change.

You can sketch your *maps of media space* using a pencil and paper. You may also develop them using a graphic program on a computer. This way you can change your diagram as your perception of your media space expands. You can also share your map of media space with others in your workgroup so they know how to find information you share. Learn to diagram the media space environments you have access to using different devices.

VISUALIZATION

People can develop models to visualize the realities they are working with.

Models may be graphic images, 3-D spatial models, 2-D locational models such as maps or plans. They may be quantitative models like cost estimates or feasibility studies often done on spreadsheets. Visualization is a key to creativity. It helps you clarify perceptions, contemplate new connections, and coordinate actions. Visualization draws upon your innate capacity to work with patterns.

Models become information objects you can interact with electronically. You can learn to transfer information directly to these models. You can also use these models as shared information objects for collaboration. This has tremendous implications for teaching and learning as well as for focusing the interaction of creative work groups.

Fig. 6.5. Visualization.   **Fig. 6.6. Direct transfer.**

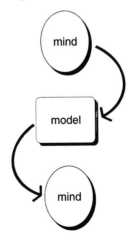

As the bandwidth of interaction widens through multimedia, it becomes easier to experience virtual reality. When reading, you may become engrossed in a story and in your mind's eye imagine you are there. When interacting electronically with multimedia as you might in a video game or with virtual reality, you can, in effect, be there. This has tremendous implications for how you can work with information. The distinction between viewing reality and viewing artificial realities is becoming more subtle.

Fig. 6.7. Realities.

reality relates to virtual reality

physical space relates to media space

CREATIVE THINKING

People can learn to use their creative capacity when working electronically.

Using descriptions of the creative process that scientists, mathematicians, and psychologists experience, Betty Edwards—who is an artist, educator, and writer—integrated them in a very understandable way. In her book *Drawing on the Artist Within*, she summarized the creative process in five stages:

1. First insight

2. Saturation

3. Incubation

4. Illumination

5. Verification

Each stage can involve varying lengths of time, depending upon what you are doing. The creative process is cyclical rather than linear. You typically cycle through many iterations.

Fig. 6.8. Edward's description of the creative process.

first insight
↓
saturation
↓
incubation
↓

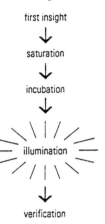

illumination
↓
verification

Fig. 6.9. Lowenfeld's description of the creative process.

preparation
↓
incubation
↓

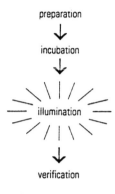

illumination
↓
verification

Fig. 6.10. Gordon's description of the creative process.

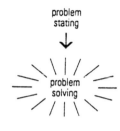

problem stating
↓
problem solving

Fig. 6.11. RSVP cycles. Adapted from *RSVP Cycles: Creative Process in the Human Environment* by Halprin.

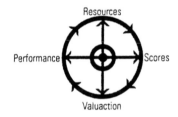

Fig. 6.12. ETC cycles. Adapted from *Experiences in Visual Thinking* by McKim.

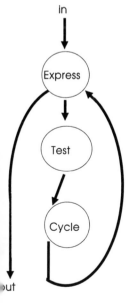

In
Express
Test
Cycle
Out

Fig. 6.13. The river metaphor. Adapted from *Design for Human Ecosystems* by Lyle.

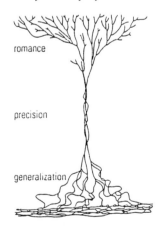

romance

precision

generalization

The *design process* used in disciplines—such as architecture and landscape architecture—usually involves:

Research (which is really problem identification and information gathering)

Analysis

Synthesis

Evaluation

You can see that this design process is really patterned after the creative processes described by others. Each discipline typically has its own rubric for describing the creative process. The approach may vary and the words used to describe the approach may be somewhat different, but the basic pattern is the same. People in many disciplines can use information objects to develop models that enable them to explore ideas electronically.

COLLABORATION

People can learn and work collaboratively in the emerging electronic information environments.

In her book *Transformations: Process and Theory*, Doreen Nelson has developed an object-oriented approach to education. She uses a model of a city as the focus for teaching students to develop their creativity. The model is also a vehicle for interconnecting subjects and teaching students a great deal about the environment. She reverses traditional learning by first immersing students in the design of an object and then drawing them into historic research that they then find relevant. The philosophy behind this approach relates to educational theories put forth by John Dewey, Hilda Taba, Benjamin Bloom, John Guilford, and Jerome Bruner. The typical framework of education tends to lose many of these ideas. Curriculum is more influenced by scheduling—organizing time and space.

As we move into electronic media space, we can transcend certain physical limitations like time and space. There are new opportunities to implement some of these educational theories. For example, one limitation of using objects—such as a model of a city or a project like those done in a design studio—is that they take up classroom space. Another is that they may be messy. And there is no place for storage. (If you can save models, you can share them with others or use them as a starting point or example for the next year's class.) The typical classroom environment does not work well for object-oriented teaching. Most classrooms must be scheduled for different groups, or used to teach different subjects, satisfying "classroom utilization formulas." Usually, there is no real time to get different groups to work together on these objects when collaboration could be desirable.

What if students and teachers create objects, like a city model, in electronic media space? The cost of purchasing computers for accessing and maintaining media space is probably less than building, maintaining, and accessing the physical classroom and studio space (which usually isn't available). You can schedule media space with much greater flexibility than you can schedule physical classroom space. You could create virtual realities for project- or object-oriented education.

Fig. 6.14. Object-oriented workgroup.

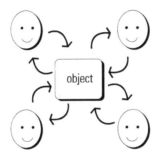

A MIND PRIMER

Students can begin to learn creative thinking skills at an early age.

How can we help school children learn these important thinking skills for the electronic age? "What is needed is a 'mind primer' for computer literacy courses in primary and secondary schools. This could help young people learn creative and critical thinking skills that they can draw upon when they use electronic media."[2] Also, you could relate what you learn from reading *Mind over Media* to information resource courses you teach. As you can see, many of these thinking skills are important for working in virtual libraries and school library media centers that are emerging. I wish you well in this endeavor. Please let me know how you might use a mind primer if it was available for courses you teach.

INTERNET: mjvonwodtke@csupomona.edu

NOTES

1. The diagrams and all portions of this article except "The Challenge" are adapted from *Mind over Media: Creative Thinking Skills for Electronic Media* (New York: McGraw-Hill, 1993), by Mark von Wodtke.

2. Ibid., 300.

7

The Information Curriculum
Teaching Concepts for the Virtual Library Environment

℞   HILDA K. WEISBURG and RUTH TOOR   ℟

Many practices found in schools today began at the close of the 19th century. As the 21st century approaches there are strong indications that education is ready for significant change. School restructuring, the impact of technology, multiculturalism, and the advent of the Age of Information are permanently altering how and what is being taught.

Numerous library media specialists have already adopted resource based instruction as the most effective way to prepare lifelong learners. Regular experience with a multiplicity of resources is obviously essential to successful information management. However the enormous amount of recoverable data, the speed at which emerging technology becomes fully developed, and the uncertainty of what is yet to come require that these resource based units be presented as part of a new curriculum—the Information Curriculum.

The Information Curriculum prepares students for selecting, interpreting, and using a flood of ideas, moving effortlessly between subject disciplines, and accessing sources from a variety of formats. It needs to be incorporated into *all* subject areas as teachers and library media specialists collaboratively plan their resource based units to develop students' critical thinking skills. Students learn to make sophisticated choices, recognizing that when dealing with complex ideas:

There is no one right answer.

There is no one correct route to finding information.

Analysis is more important than rote memory.

Their own purpose defines the value of a specific piece of information.

Information needs change during a research project.

These thinking skills, which accustom students to identifying general principles rather than remembering rote facts, are part of the Ten Concepts that form the basis of the Information Curriculum.

Library activities that focus on specifics, where students can find the right answer if they follow directions, don't prepare them for real life. A few generic principles coupled with some regular experience in making choices and evaluating information are much more effective.

The world of the future will undoubtedly include ever-widening access to resources with increasingly efficient search mechanisms. The entire world of libraries will be available from people's homes. How will users know where to begin?

You must prepare students with a curriculum based on generic principles applicable to any situation. The Information Curriculum has at its core Ten Concepts that form the basis for understanding and using libraries—however the future defines them—and efficiently managing the information they contain.

TEN CONCEPTS

Concept 1: A shared pool of materials benefits everyone.

Concept 2: Library materials are arranged by subject.

Concept 3: Reference materials are available for all subjects.

Concept 4: Recognition of the arrangement of a resource speeds access to its information.

Concept 5: Indexes are the major key to locating information rapidly.

Concept 6: Not all information is equal.

Concept 7: Timeliness of information is an important consideration.

Concept 8: Information may carry bias.

Concept 9: Research requires both thinking and communicating.

Concept 10: Voluntary reading is a basis for building knowledge.

IMPLICATIONS OF THE CONCEPTS

Concept 1:
A Shared Pool of Materials Benefits Everyone

Basic to the most traditional as well as the most futuristic attitude is the idea that sharing resources and ideas benefits everyone. This concept is fundamental whether it concerns the orientation given to kindergartners (or preschoolers) when children learn to recognize that they, as individuals, do not own the books but get to borrow them or the complexities of interlibrary loan through networks and Internet access. It also incorporates the realization that the individual has obligations. The responsibilities of being part of a group, whether they refer to keeping books clean and returning them on time or fulfilling network membership commitments, must be accepted by all.

Concept 2:
Library Materials Are Arranged by Subject

Subjects are the unifying principle behind library arrangement. Telling students that books are either fiction or nonfiction and they can recognize the difference because nonfiction has numbers leads to confusion. Even elementary graders observe that fairy tales are not true yet have Dewey numbers. Rather than being taught the individual differences of every library they use, students must recognize their similarities and understand that any variations arise out of each library's efforts to meet user needs.

Concept 3:
Reference Materials Are Available for All Subjects

Traditional discussions of reference materials focus on encyclopedias, dictionaries, atlases, and almanacs as though they encompass the entire category. Good research skills require that students understand general and subject-specific reference resources. This concept is introduced from the earliest grades by identifying the reference materials in the subject area being explored (for an animal unit, *The New Book of Popular Science* and/or the more specific *Encyclopedia of Mammals*) and contrasting them with general reference materials (*The World Book Encyclopedia*). Students must learn when each type is more appropriate and what differences they can expect to find.

Concept 4:
Recognition of the Arrangement of a Resource Speeds Access to Its Information

While this statement incorporates the old "parts of a book" skill, the concept itself is more general. Students at all levels must use textual clues and format structure to determine the best and fastest route to their information. Concept 4 applies equally to print and nonprint resources. Making lists of directions for all computer databases in the media center is not helpful in the long run. Students must learn to read screens and adapt their approach to the idiosyncrasies of each. Early identification of helpful appendices, use of color blocks, or any other way of organizing devised by the publisher improves the speed and quality of a search.

Concept 5:
Indexes Are the Major Key to Locating Information Rapidly

The ability to identify and understand indexes, whether print or computer-based, is essential to research. Instead of spending time teaching their use with specific encyclopedias and periodicals, the focus remains on the general concept. Students must know what an index does and realize that its purpose remains the same regardless of format.

Concept 6:
Not All Information Is Equal

This is the first of three concepts that deal with the criteria needed for evaluating information to use it efficiently. Even the youngest student can learn to question the accuracy of a source. Just because something appears in print—or on a screen—is no guarantee that it is factual. Students must become aware that different sources have varying levels of credibility.

Concept 7:
Timeliness of Information Is an Important Consideration

Nothing is as old as yesterday's news. Even fairly stable topics need to be checked for current information. From the earliest grades students must become alert to copyright dates and other indicators to ensure they have located the most recent data and analyses.

Concept 8:
Information May Carry Bias

A subtle but important skill is the ability to identify when information is being used to promote a particular point of view. Not only must students be able to recognize that something is slanted, whether in print or visual media, but to be efficient users of information they must also know how to employ data to send their own messages.

Concept 9:
Research Requires Both Thinking and Communicating

The complexities of research demand use of all the skills students have acquired throughout their education. The true test of what they have learned should cover not only the gathering of information but also demonstrate students' ability to communicate their findings to others.

Concept 10:
Voluntary Reading Is a Basis
for Building Knowledge

Reading for pleasure is a vital component of the Information Curriculum. While research is focused on a specific target, random recreational reading builds background, connections, and associations that are the basis of all knowledge.

END PRODUCTS, INFORMATION SHEETS, AND GUIDED INQUIRY

The Ten Concepts that form the framework of the new curriculum must be accompanied by changes in the way you teach. As you develop units within the Information Curriculum the decisions you make at three different stages directly influence the success of resource based instruction.

End products the teacher requires determine:
    extent of student searches.
    amount of critical thinking.
    number of learning styles addressed.

Jointly prepared *information sheets* determine:
    scope of strategies and choices.
    degree of information management.
    level of student involvement.

Careful use of *guided inquiry questions* determine how well students think through and solve problems.

End Products

After identifying unit objectives you and the teacher must decide on an end product to accurately evaluate learner outcomes. What elements should be considered? If you are implementing the Information Curriculum, students need numerous opportunities to make choices, establish criteria for selecting facts, and effectively present results using different communication skills.

The first two elements, choosing sources and setting criteria, require students to develop search strategies and manage information, so end products should not be too restrictive. For an animal unit everyone should not work on the same animal or classification. Limited resources would force students to choose what is readily available rather than have the opportunity to evaluate among alternatives. End products should present not only specific data (size, location, and habitat) but also more open questions that require critical thinking (What would happen if the animal became extinct? How are black and brown bears similar or different?).

In making choices about which resource to use and the specifics to extract, students learn to set criteria for accuracy and relevance. At the same time they have the freedom to develop their own preferences for sources based on their learning styles. (Do they like or dislike working with computer databases? Do pictures add or distract?)

The end product is normally the research presentation. Classically it is a report or term paper. Although this format easily serves as an evaluation, other possibilities should be kept in mind.

Since teaching is the best way to learn and civilization has always thrived on wide dissemination of information, why limit students' work to one reader? The end product should incorporate some means of sharing results with others, again encompassing different learning styles.

Several end products can be used for a single unit. If a teacher's idea seems too restrictive, you can suggest additional possibilities as you jointly develop the project.

Information Sheets

When you and the teacher collaboratively plan a resource based unit, information sheets help students stay focused on the project. Unlike traditional worksheets these never have fill-in-the-blank or multiple-choice questions. Most of the time several answers are possible although some choices may be better than others. Not a pathfinder, these do not direct students to a prescribed sequence of tools, although they may suggest possible entry terms to get their thinking started. What these information sheets do is:

Point toward the type of information needed

Outline a search strategy

Identify student choices

Target a search

Suggest ways to present results

An information sheet might ask for the latest facts or a graphic such as a chart. It may suggest a sequence of steps in a strategy (locate an overview of the issue, note main concepts, etc.).

Open-ended queries encourage judgments about findings that may lead students to further searches. Asking, "How many solutions can you find for this issue?" and/or "Which is the best way to deal with this problem? Why do you think so?" calls forth a personal, reasoned reaction to their research.

Giving students a list of entry terms begins the brainstorming for additional ones. This list readies them to adapt and revise their searches depending on whatever source they are using.

Information sheets may include several choices for the final presentation. Students should be aware how they will use their research. The questions you and the teacher devise will keep them pointed in the right direction.

Guided Inquiry

One of the most difficult aspects of implementing the Information Curriculum involves changing your own teaching. You want students to learn how to use their minds, think problems through, and develop workable solutions. Telling them what to do only encourages rote skills and does not address higher order thinking.

Questioning students is not new, but all too often these are oral tests. The required answers are frequently one word. In essence what you are doing is challenging them to recall or guess what you want them to say.

To develop students' critical thinking skills you have to stop telling and start asking. But the questions must be as thought provoking and open-ended as possible. Instead of saying, "What do you have to do to find information in the encyclopedia?" and accepting only the answer, "Look in the index volume," consider asking, "What are some good techniques for getting the information you need from encyclopedias?" Their answers will include pictures, diagrams, typeface, maps, etc. As a suggestion is offered, have that student explain how it helps. Sum up responses as a transition into the next part of the lesson and if no one mentions an index, include it in your wind-up.

An alternative, ensuring that students recognize the importance of the index, is to pose the question and immediately answer, "My first stop is the index." Then let them tell you why and continue with other possibilities.

To improve your skill in guided inquiry, try listening to yourself as you present lessons. See if others in the class can reason the problems out before giving the answers. If you find yourself asking for a rote response, pause and restate. It is not easy to break old habits, but if you tune in to what you are saying you will develop the knack and be amazed at how much your students are learning.

SUMMARY

Change is always difficult, but many library media specialists have already recognized the need to make adjustments in response to new technological developments in the Information Age. Resource based instruction is just the first step. As your experience using it grows, you realize that methods and techniques must be attuned to expanding not inhibiting opportunities for critical thinking. Outcomes and processes—end products and the worksheets and guided inquiry questions that lead to them—must be analyzed carefully to help students develop the strategies necessary to manage information.

These lessons should be set within a new curriculum, one that provides guidelines rather than fixed rules. The ideas behind the Ten Concepts have always been part of library instruction but organizing them into general principles changes your perspective about the way you present units. Now students can develop a working frame of reference to last a lifetime.

8

The Process of Learning from Information[1]

CAROL COLLIER KUHLTHAU

THE INFORMATION-AGE SCHOOL LIBRARY

The major challenge of the information-age school is to educate children for living and learning in an information-rich environment. One of the most important abilities students can acquire to function in that information-rich environment is an understanding of the process of learning. A sense of this process enables students to apply the wide range of skills they develop during their years of schooling in everyday living. Without a sense of process, students don't see the similarities in disparate disciplines, making it difficult to transfer skills from one situation to another. Library media programs need to be restructured to serve the information-age school and instill in students using a variety of sources of information a sense of the process of learning.

Over the past 30 years, school librarianship became particularly attuned to the changing needs of the local community and society-at-large. This well-established pattern of response places us in an excellent position to address the challenges of the information age, difficult challenges upon which we must act without delay and with great resolve and competence.

It may be helpful, at this point, to take stock of the accomplishments in school librarianship over the past 30 years that form the basis on which to build for the future. In the sixties, the foundational concepts of school libraries were established, incorporating a specialized facility, staff, and collection to accommodate the learning objectives of the school. The school library was identified as different from the public library in that the collection reflected the curriculum, and the professional staff were trained as teachers as well as librarians. In the seventies, school librarianship fostered integration of a variety of media across the curriculum, and the concept of a library media program encompassing reading incentives and library skills instruction emerged. In the eighties, the library media program was expanded to incorporate the concepts of instructional design, resource-based learning, and integration with the curriculum. By the mid-eighties, the computer was commonplace bringing major new concepts to school librarianship, including automating the collection and various other new computer applications. These innovations demanded considerable attention and time and we are still in the midst of this transition. However, it is imperative that these demands do not distract us from our newest challenge, the task of promoting student learning in the information age.

95

The nineties have brought important new concepts to school librarianship. The self-contained collection is giving way to an extensive information network and the virtual library. The computer has made a wide variety of resources readily available, creating an information-rich environment, and now the school library program must concentrate on finding ways to use this information effectively. The problem of information overload has become common, and devising ways of seeking meaning is essential.

Information literacy is an expansion of library skills. Library skills prepare students to locate materials in a library. Information prepares students to learn in an information-rich environment. Information literacy encompasses lifelong learning and the application of information skills to everyday living. Therefore, the school library program must be prepared to respond to the need and help students gain information literacy.

The process of learning from information is the key concept for the school library media center in the information-age school. Yet in many instances, process may be neglected by library media specialists who are too firmly tied to the methods of the past or are distracted by the demands of getting the technology up and running. Neglecting to teach students about process in research and learning leaves them without the essential holistic concepts for transferring learning to real-life situations. A concept of process is an essential component in restructuring library media programs for the information-age school.

PROCESS LEARNING

Author David Macaulay, in his acceptance speech as winner of the 1991 Caldecott Medal, made a plea for exposing children to process. He explained the importance of process in his life work and described how his parents were always making things and involving him in the process of creating. He expressed grave concern for today's children, who confront most things fully constructed and have little opportunity to experience process. "It is now possible for almost any child to get through childhood without any knowledge whatsoever of the P-word (process) and without suffering the slightest case of curiosity" (1991, 340-47).

In a series of studies on the student's perspective of the information search process, my own research has discovered a similar problem in library research (Kuhlthau 1989). Students commonly approach their own library research as if there was only one right answer and one perfect project. They often are not engaged in a process of using information to construct their own learning. My studies show that developing an understanding of the constructive process through guided self-awareness substantially increases students' confidence and competence in learning from information. The following case illustrates the importance of understanding the process of library research (Kuhlthau 1988).

The subject of case study was a high school student for whom English was a second language. Because he was learning a new language, he felt disadvantaged academically and was determined to find ways to compete successfully in an academic environment. He volunteered for a case study, the first in the series of studies I conducted on the information search process. He explained that he thought he might learn something about library research that would help him in college. When interviewed after completion of four years of undergraduate work, he explained the impact of his understanding of process in this way:

I had more exposure to research papers than most high school students. By working with [the author] I learned not to panic if it doesn't all fall in together the first day you walk into the library. I had a lot of friends in college who were panicked at doing a research paper. I'll welcome a research paper any day, regardless of the subject. To tell you the truth, I haven't come across any of my peers who think like that, not a one. When my roommate's research paper was due last semester, I helped him with it. He doesn't even know what he is afraid of, afraid of not finding the one article that is going to make his paper? I'll worry about a paper because things don't fall into place but it's not the kind of thing I lose sleep over. I've learned to accept that this is the way it works. Tomorrow I'll read this over and some parts will fall into place and some still won't. If not, I'll talk to the professor. The mind doesn't take everything and put it into order automatically, and that's it. Understanding that is the biggest help. (Kuhlthau 1988, 282)

This student had learned to anticipate the learning process inherent in library research and had developed strategies for coping with the uncertainty and confusion he experienced. What is unfortunate is the difficulty he observed in other students who had not been exposed to their own process of learning in library research assignments in prior schooling. When interviewed again four years later, this student was employed by a stock analysis firm to compile reports on various corporations. He explained that he can never have too much information because he seeks a thread or theme as a focus to provide a story or narrative in the information he gathers. In this way he had developed a strategy for addressing information overload. Process gave him a way to work through masses of information. Learning to find a focus gave him a frame for seeking meaning and making sense. He understood that his main task was to construct meaning from the information he gathered, and he was confident that he could do this. In other words, he was information literate.

THE INFORMATION SEARCH PROCESS

My studies demonstrate the importance of teaching the information search process rather than assuming that students will acquire an understanding of the process on their own. The information-age school must create an environment in which students can experience the information search process and provide situations where they can reflect and become aware of their own process. Through reflection on their own experiences, students internalize the process for transference to other situations.

A model of the information search process, developed from the findings of five studies, serves as a guide for designing instructional programs. In brief, the information search process may be thought of as occurring in six stages: initiation, selection, exploration, formulation, collection, and presentation. The stages are named for the primary task at each point in the process.

Initiation marks the beginning of the process, when the assignment is first introduced. Students are frequently puzzled by the task and uncertain as to how to proceed. Thoughts are commonly centered externally on "What does the teacher want?" and not internally on "What do I know?" and "What do I want to know and learn?"

Selection is a time for identifying a general idea for investigation; it is often accompanied by a sense of optimism at accomplishing the task at hand. Some students may take more time at this task than others, and those who do not select quickly can become anxious at being behind the group. Point out to students that the pace of the information search process varies greatly from person to person and from problem to problem. The only time a whole group of students will be together is at initiation and presentation.

Exploration is unexpectedly the most difficult of the entire process. After the general topic has been selected students expect to be able to move on to collecting information and to preparing to present. However, exploration, as the name indicates, is a more varied and complex task. At this point, students' task is to explore information to determine a focus for their research. They need to read and reflect to learn enough about the general topic or problem to form a personal perspective or focus for their work. Confidence can be expected to drop sharply during this stage before increasing gradually. As students encounter inconsistent, incompatible information that does not match their expectations, they often begin to doubt the appropriateness of the topic, the adequacy of the information sources, and their own ability to accomplish the assignment. This is to be expected and they need to concentrate on exploring information to form a focus for their research rather than collecting information to support a thesis. One of the most common mistakes in library research is to confuse the stages of exploration and collection (step 5) and therefore to apply collection strategies in the exploration stage. When these two stages are confused, students run into all kinds of problems including writing blocks, because they haven't formed a personal perspective, and plagiarism, because at this stage, they have little sense of meaning.

Formulation is conceptually the most important stage in the information search process, during which the central cognitive task of the process is accomplished, and the student forms a personal perspective or sense of the meaning of the information encountered. At this time the student begins to move from uncertainty to understanding. The focus provides a guiding idea, a theme, or a thread, on which to base the collection of information. The focus provides the frame for constructing a story or narrative using the information that is gathered. Formulating a focus gives the student a strategy for selecting information from an information-rich environment and is necessary in using information rather than merely locating information. During the formulation stage, students are actively engaged in using information to create meaning that involves thinking, reflecting, interpreting, connecting, and extending.

In the fifth stage, *collection*, the task is to gather information that defines and supports the focus formed in the prior stage. The focus is further shaped and clarified during this stage as connections and extensions are made from the information gathered. The narrative begins to take shape. Many of the strategies used in traditional library searching, are helpful at this point and can be adapted to the technological environment such as subject searching and detailed notetaking.

Presentation is the completion of the narrative describing the focused perspective of the topic and to prepare to present the new learning to the intended audience. This can be a difficult stage if little formulation has taken place during the information search process. One student who had not done sufficient formulation during the process described a serious writing block:

I had a general idea not a specific focus, but an idea. As I was writing, I didn't know what my focus was. When I was finished, I didn't know what my focus was. My teacher says she doesn't know what my focus was. I don't think I ever acquired a focus. It was an impossible paper to write. I would just sit there and say, "I'm stuck." There was no outline because there was no focus and there was nothing to complete. If I learned anything from that paper it is, you have to have a focus. You have to have something to center on. You can't just have a topic. You should have an idea when you start. I had a topic but I didn't know what I wanted to do with it. I figured that when I did my research it would focus in. But I didn't let it. I kept saying "this is interesting and this is interesting and I'll just smush it altogether." It didn't work out. (Kuhlthau 1994, 55)

Writing blocks are commonly indicative of thinking blocks. Research on the writing process has revolutionized the way children learn to write. However, the writing process centers on writing from what is already known and in the long-term memory (Stotsky 1990). Research on the information search process addresses how information is used to form constructs and to provide something to write about. The information search process concentrates on learning from information prior to and during the prewriting stage of the writing process and needs to be incorporated into established writing process instruction.

As students learn to write across the curriculum they can also learn how to learn from information across the curriculum. Through problem-initiated instruction they can acquire skills for addressing problems in the disciplines of science, history, social studies, mathematics, literature, and language. In addition, the audience for student research can be expanded beyond the teacher to the class, the school, and the community.

In an information-age school student use of information for learning needs to be brought to the center of the instructional program. Student research is no longer merely an enrichment activity, but is an important way to learn in preparation for living and working in an information-rich environment. Incorporating these concepts into the library media program calls for an information search process approach (ISPA) to information skills instruction.

UNDERLYING CONCEPTS OF THE ISPA

The ISPA has become well established in many schools in the United States, Canada, Sweden, and other countries. The three main research findings from the basic concepts in the ISPA are: 1) Information searching is a process over time rather than a single event; 2) information searching is a complex, holistic experience rather than a simple, single activity; and 3) at first, information searching usually increases rather than decreases uncertainty.

The ISPA introduces students to the process of information seeking and strives to develop skills for using a variety of sources of information for learning across the curriculum. Based on the model of the information search process, it guides students through each stage in the process, implementing useful strategies along the way.

Students experience the information search process holistically with an interplay of thoughts, feelings, and actions. Common patterns of thinking, feeling, and acting are characteristic in each stage. These studies were among the first to investigate the affective aspects of students' feelings during the process of information seeking and use along with the cognitive and physical aspects. One of the most surprising findings was the discovery of a sharp increase in uncertainty and decrease in confidence.

Uncertainty is a basic underlying principle of the ISPA. Uncertainty is not only to be accepted in the information search process but to be expected as a normal condition. Students need to clearly understand that "the mind doesn't take everything and put it into order automatically, and that's it." They need to develop strategies for using information for thinking and formulating to seek meaning during the information search process.

Of course, the developmental level of the students is an important consideration when adopting an ISPA. All elementary and secondary school children can learn from a variety of sources of information. However, the level of abstraction that they are equipped to handle will depend on their experience and will develop as they mature (Kuhlthau 1981). The program for younger children should center around concrete information and straightforward research topics and problems. Older children can work with more abstract ideas, formulating their own focused perspective on the information they gather. It is a serious error to require one research assignment for all age children. There is a difference in the information use of younger and older children that needs to be taken into account when planning an ISPA. A transition threshold seems to occur around 11 or 12 years of age, although this may vary somewhat individually or culturally.

ABILITIES FOR LEARNING FROM A VARIETY OF SOURCES OF INFORMATION

There are some basic abilities for using information that young children can learn and that older children find extremely useful. When children practice these abilities at an early age, they build a solid foundation for using information as they mature and grow. Four basic abilities of information use are recalling, summarizing, paraphrasing, and extending.

Recalling is thinking back over the information that has been gathered and read to pick certain parts and features that stand out in the mind. Memory plays a critical role in information use and is an important part of thinking about information at an early age. Recall can be highly selective, differing from one child to another. When asking a child to recall there should be room for more than one answer. What is recalled depends to a large extent on the experience of the child and the child's former constructs.

Summarizing is capsulizing information to draw out salient points. It involves organizing ideas and placing them in a meaningful place. The task of summarizing is to choose what is important, pertinent, and significant from an individual view. Young children are being asked to summarize when they are directed to identify the main points of a passage. Rather than expecting that all students name the same ideas, encourage them to identify what seems important or interesting or surprising to them. In this way, they are learning to use information for thinking about ideas in a creative, personal way.

Paraphrasing is retelling in one's own words what has been encountered in resources. The use of individual language fosters formulation and prepares information for application. The concept behind paraphrasing is that the child's words are as acceptable as the author's and are more appropriate under certain circumstances. The child is encouraged to break away from the text to tell the story in his or her own way. This also helps the child feel mastery and understanding of the information. When paraphrasing is not valued, copying and plagiarism often result. Children's retelling or paraphrasing needs to be valued and encouraged from the earliest age. Assignments should require paraphrasing ideas rather than result from a contrived directive that prompts copying a text word for word.

Extending is taking ideas from sources and fitting them in with what one already knows. Extending also involves making connections between ideas within information and with information from other sources. In this way, the child's thoughts about a topic or problem are extended. Extending also encompasses interpreting information and applying it to a problem in the creative process of using information.

These four abilities are interconnected in the active process of seeking meaning. Recalling is closely related to summarizing. Paraphrasing is telling what is recalled and summarized. Paraphrasing may be used to enable recall as one point cues another while the telling occurs. In a similar way paraphrasing may enable summarizing as the story unfolds in the act of telling.

STRATEGIES FOR THE ISPA

Students can learn to apply the following strategies in the ISPA: collaborating, continuing, conversing, charting, and composing.

Collaborating. A team approach to library research more closely matches real world information seeking tasks. Collaborative strategies such as brainstorming, delegating, networking, and integrating are productive activities for information seeking and develop abilities valued in the workplace. Instruction that promotes collaboration in the process of information seeking and use builds skills and understanding that transfer to other situations of information need.

Continuing. Continuing looks at information problems rather than questions that can be answered with a single source. Information seeking involves construction in which the student actively pursues understanding and meaning from the information encountered over a period of time. Continuing responds to students' complex, dynamic learning process. Instruction that continues throughout the information search process not only guides students in one specific research assignment but also establishes transferable process skills. Students are led to view information seeking as a constructive process and to know that exploration and formulation are essential tasks for bringing order to uncertainty through personal understanding.

Continuing also addresses the concept of "enough." It's important to understand what is enough information for closure and presentation. What is enough was a relatively simple notion when a person could gather all there was to know on a topic, but it is quite a different matter in the present-day information environment. Understanding what is enough is essential for making sense of information around us, for seeking meaning in a quantity of information by determining what one needs to know and by formulating a perspective. The information search process treats enough as what is enough to make sense for oneself.

Continuing strategies enable students to decide what is enough to recognize an information need, to explore a general topic, to formulate a specific focus, to gather information pertaining to the specific focus, to prepare to share what has been learned, or to solve a problem. Continuing strategies support students throughout the information search process and guide them in using information for learning each stage of the process.

Conversing. Conversing encourages students to discuss the information search process from their own particular perspective. Students collaborate and learn through conversations with their peers about the information they are encountering and the ideas they are developing.

Library media specialists may encourage dialogue by drawing upon the students' dynamic process through invitational, exploratory questioning: What ideas seem important to you? What questions do you have? What problems are emerging? What is the focus of your thinking? What are the guiding ideas for your search? What are the gaps in your thinking? What inconsistencies do you notice in the information you have encountered?

Conversing gives the library media specialist an opportunity to listen to the student and to recommend appropriate strategies for working through the process. Diagnosis of the stage of the process the student is in is important as formulation of a focused perspective is the turning point in the search. The library media specialist recommends different strategies before and after the formulation of a focus. Prior to formulation a more invitational approach to searching is recommended; there might need to be more exploratory reading and reflecting to better understand the problem. Following formulation a more focused approach of documenting and organizing is recommended to solve the problem.

Charting. The timeline of the information search process developed in the studies may be adopted as an instrument for illustrating the overall process to students. The diagram enables students to visualize a sequence of stages in information-seeking and to identify the stage that the students are working on. The timeline can be simply drawn on a piece of paper or prepared as a formal handout. The objective is for students to understand the process and to decide at what stage they would place themselves in the sequence.

Timelines and flowcharts may be adapted for guiding students in charting their own searches. These instruments are most effective for reviewing a recently completed search with a student and reflecting on what went well and what might be improved. They may also be used as planning instruments. Students may also chart their ideas and organize their thoughts in the form of concept maps and graphic organizers at critical points in the information search process. Charting used in this way promotes constructive learning.

Composing. Composing promotes thinking, and journal writing is an excellent strategy for advancing formulation in the information search process. Library media specialists may recommend that students keep a research journal in which they record ideas, questions, and connections as they progress through their search. Writing in a research journal is much more comprehensive than jotting notes. The journal is started when the project is initiated, but the purpose changes as the search progresses. Students are instructed to set aside a minimum of 10 to 15 minutes each day to write about their problems or topics. The main objective of a research journal is to serve as a tool for formulating thoughts and developing constructs.

ENABLERS AND INHIBITORS OF ISPA

Some library media specialists have had great success in implementing an ISPA; others have not been as productive. In a study conducted over a period of three years I investigated this variation in results (Kuhlthau 1993a, 1993b). The study revealed some inhibitors and enablers in the implementation of a process approach. Not all schools are organized to accommodate the constructive process of students. Some were better prepared for implementation than others. Participants in faltering programs cited three primary inhibitors: lack of time, confusion of roles, and poorly designed research assignments.

The four basic enablers identified in libraries reporting successful implementation of a process approach were: a team approach to library services, a mutually held constructivist view of information-seeking, a shared commitment to instructing and guiding in skills for lifelong learning, and competence in designing process strategies. A process approach to information skills was revealed as a team effort. The team was committed to improving information use. The notion of assisting and counseling students in the constructive process of information-seeking provided a solid theoretical basis for building library services and for developing a process approach to information-seeking.

CONCLUSION

The information-age school library prepares children for productive living in an information-rich environment. Library media programs need to be restructured to serve the information-age school. Our mission is for every child to have the opportunity to become information literate. The central goal of the restructured library media program is to develop ability in the process of learning from a variety of sources of information in each subject in the curriculum.

This is the essential piece to the puzzle that is missing in many efforts to restructure education of the twenty-first century. Failing to prepare students for learning in an information-rich environment is to fail to meet the challenge of education today. The school library as the information center of the information-age school is the laboratory for learning essential abilities for living in the information society. It is time for school librarians worldwide to play a central role in creating information-age schools for their local communities.

NOTE

1. Reprinted from *School Libraries Worldwide*, vol. 1, no. 1, January 1995, pp. 1-12.

REFERENCES

Kuhlthau, Carol Collier. (1981). *School Librarian's Grade-by-Grade Activities Program: A Complete Sequential Skills Plan for Grades K-8*. West Nyack, NY: Center for Applied Research in Education.

———. (1988). "Longitudinal Case Studies of the Information Search Process of Users in Libraries." *Library and Information Science Research* 10, no. 3: 257-304.

———. (1989). "Information Search Process: A Summary of Research and Implications for School Library Media Programs." *School Library Media Quarterly* 18, no. 5: 19-25.

———. (1993a). "Implementing a Process Approach to Information Skills: A Study Identifying Indicators of Success in Library Media Programs." *School Library Media Quarterly* 21, no. 1: 11-18.

———. (1993b). *Seeking Meaning: A Process Approach to Library and Information Services.* Norwood, NJ: Ablex.

———. (1994). *Teaching the Library Research Process*, 2d ed. Metuchen, NJ: Scarecrow.

Macaulay, David. 1991. "Caldecott Acceptance Speech." *Journal of Youth Service in Libraries* 4, no. 4: 340-47.

Stotsky, S. 1990. "On Planning and Writing Plans." *College and Composition and Communication* 41, no. 1: 37-57.

Part III

Examples of Implementation

9

Access to Computer Telecommunications Through CORE/Internet at the Pleasant Valley High School
A Letter to Readers

ଝ PETER MILBURY ℘

Dear Peter Milbury:

Your name is quite well known as one of the administrators of the popular LM_NET listserv. We wonder if you would give our readers a picture of how you got started in the world of the Internet as so many others are facing the same challenge.

—the editors

Dear Readers:

At Pleasant Valley High School (grades 9-12), in Chico, California, computer technology, and telecommunications in particular, is an integral part of our library program and the school's curriculum. The library technology center is the school's primary computer telecommunications gateway. Here, students may use the CD-ROM databases on our PC-based local area network. They may create reports, papers, and presentations on our student Macintosh network or make use of our audio-visual media, books, and other materials in the reading room or career center. One of the most exciting new resources, however, is access to the Internet.

More than a third of our teachers and three-fourths of our administrators now have accounts on CORE (California Online Resources for Education) the wide area network and gateway to the Internet for California's public schools. More than a hundred Pleasant Valley High School students also have accounts on CORE/Internet. They use Internet resources independently and in class assignments. CORE accounts are currently available free to California educators. Students may also have accounts, with teacher sponsorship. Access to CORE/Internet at Pleasant Valley High is through modem, although we expect to have a direct link installed during the 1994-95 school year.

Chico is a rural community of approximately 80,000 people, 190 miles northeast of San Francisco, and 90 miles north of Sacramento, at the western edge of the Sierra Mountains. We are a college town, and also a farming and commercial center for the region. Therefore contact and connections with the urban areas of our state, and with the rest of the country and world are of great benefit to our staff and students. Pleasant Valley is one of two four-year comprehensive high schools in Chico Unified School District, which also includes two junior highs, 14 elementary schools, and a small alternative high school.

Through the good graces and support of Pleasant Valley High principal, Mr. Robert Cranston, I have been exploring the Internet since fall 1990, when I joined the P.V. staff as the school's library media specialist. I was hired just as the school and district were formulating plans for the construction of a new library at P.V. High. Mr. Cranston and I have worked very closely during the past several years as those plans have developed and construction has started.

We feel assured that our students will have the very best technology available, as part of a library media program that is at the heart of the school's curriculum. The Internet is at the heart of our design, with access available at all of the library's networked computers. As we grow into a school-wide LAN, the Internet will also be available to students and teachers in the classrooms. This wide use of the Internet, though, would not be part of our plan if I had not been able, as part of my daily routine, to learn about this innovative technology, and then have the opportunity to share my knowledge with our staff and students.

Shortly after being hired I became the first faculty member at Pleasant Valley High to obtain Internet access, through an account with CORE. I am indeed fortunate, because I am regularly able to use time during the day to log-on to CORE and explore the Internet. I started during a time when there were very few Internet resources available for K-12 schools, and there were none of the wonderful Internet guidebooks now available. (Ed Krol's *Hitch-hiker's Guide to the Internet* was available by FTP, but we did not have FTP on CORE.) Neither were there network utilities such as Gopher, Veronica, Mosaic, WAIS, WorldWideWeb, or other aids to Internet use and navigation.

As library media specialist I had a flexibility of schedule unavailable to teachers, and was able to dial-up and go online frequently, when other library activities allowed. I had time to explore and make use of many resources that were available through Telnet (mostly Campus Wide Information Systems) and e-mail (to join discussion groups), which were the only access points to the Internet resources at that time. Toward the end of my first "Internet year," CORE obtained FTP access, and I started to make use of that protocol to obtain applications and information files, which I shared with my colleagues and students.

My interest in the Internet grew as I saw its potential for use in the K-12 setting. I soon made a point of moving my desk, with computer and modem, out of my office to the floor of the reading room. Thus I was able to go online, and still be available to my students when they needed help. I was also able to publicly model a behavior about which other teachers and students were curi-ous. It gave me an opportunity to tell them about the wonders of the Internet, and to encourage them to try it also. I soon made it a regular habit to download interesting and useful information and give copies to teachers and administrators who might use them.

As I gained confidence and skills, and as resources suitable for our students and staff became more plentiful on the Internet, I started offering occasional workshops for our staff and others in the district. Gradually, more and more colleagues obtained CORE/Internet accounts, as did students. In the 1993-94 school year I was appointed Mentor Teacher by Chico Unified School District. My special focus has been computer telecommunications. For the past two years I have offered a regular series of training sessions for our staff and others in our district. This group is called the "Internet Users Group." We meet twice each month after school to go online and share information about CORE/Internet.

Some of the regular participants in this group have been clerical, technical, and administrative staff from our district office. This has been a great benefit, as they have taken an active interest in the development of a district-wide network, and we have been able to work closely together in this undertaking. We are currently building a new library technology center at Pleasant Valley High, and many of the district office people who have attended my classes are involved in the creation of that facility. Their special interest in technology through computer telecommunications has been a great asset to us during the planning and construction.

However, my main focus is on learning about the many free resources of CORE/Internet. In the summer of 1992 I joined in an Internet venture with Syracuse professor and director of the ERIC Clearinghouse on Information and Technology, Dr. Michael Eisenberg. We established an Internet e-mail discussion group for school library media professionals, called LM_NET. I am regularly in contact through e-mail communications with a group of about two thousand school librarians, worldwide. This discussion group is an excellent resource whenever I have questions about a wide variety of matters relating to library and curriculum matters. I have frequently used this virtual community to answer questions for our administrators and my colleagues about a wide range of subjects and problems.

One of the first persons on our staff to make use of the Internet was our German language teacher. During my first two years using the Internet, she and I worked together often. My role was to help her make the initial overseas and domestic contacts, introduce her to computer telecommunications, and help her obtain an account with CORE. Now she handles most of the communicating herself. She has had some of her students corresponding with high school students in Germany, Austria, and Pittsburgh, Pennsylvania, using e-mail. The students are excited about the results. It is quite an incentive, and they have been told that their use of German is quite good. That made them very happy! In fact, it resulted in the visit to our town by one of the German students' e-mail "keypals." Another use of the Internet by German students has been to connect with libraries and information services in Germany. They obtain bibliographic and textual information for reports.

Projects with e-mail keypals can be frustrating, as the students don't always answer back. And there are not enough students on the German side to match up with all of our students. I am searching for other schools in German-speaking countries, in the hope that we can connect with more students. However, a new program sponsored by the German Consulate in San Francisco offers a great amount of support for linking American and German students through e-mail. Both of our German teachers are involved in their program.

Another early Internet resource that appealed to our staff was the free CNN Newsroom learning package. This consists of a daily 15 minute TV news broadcast and four-page study guide. It is prepared especially for secondary school teachers and students. Permission is given for teachers to freely tape and use the broadcast in their classrooms. I tape the TV program each night off CNN. Each morning I have the tape available for our American Government teacher, along with the study guide, downloaded from CORE/Internet. The Study Guide contains an overview of the broadcast, as well as a set of discussion questions, suggested classroom activities, student handouts, terminology, and recommended readings.

Our P.E. Department Chair was also an early CORE/Internet participant. She uses it to gain access to the Physical Education Bulletin Board, which has lesson and unit plans for school sports and physical education classes, as well as other related resources. She is also starting to use e-mail to communicate with other P.E.teachers throughout the state. Our P.E. Department Chair is another telecommunications designated "Mentor Teacher," and is responsible for providing staff development to other P.E. teachers in our district. She and I have given several telecommunications sessions to P.E. teachers' student teachers at California State University, Chico.

Our science department chair was another of the early CORE/Internet users among our staff. He makes use of the NASA Spacelink and other Internet science resources. He is now an old hand at exploring Internet resources, especially those related to space science, which is a personal interest for him. He has registered his classes to participate in net-wide data gathering projects. Other science teachers also have CORE accounts and are in the planning stages for using various Internet resources in their classes. I have lost track of all the things they are doing. I do know that they are active and excited Internet navigators.

One of the most active and intensive users of the library technology and our CORE/Internet resources are the students and teachers of an innovative class known as Project Icarus. This is an interdisciplinary science-humanties class, using problem-based learning strategies. Students are expected to make regular use of computer-based technology for their research, reports, and presentations. I was involved in the design of the curriculum, which is a joint project with six other high schools in Butte County, where Chico is located. Students and teachers in this project have CORE/Internet accounts, and receive Internet training along with other technology training as part of the class. CORE has allowed us to establish two conferences in its conference area, one for teachers to post information about related Internet resources, and another for students to discuss their experiences and make contact with one another.

I also have been able to register for an account with ATI-Net, based at California State University, Fresno. This is a very rich agriculture database with an extremely wide variety of information. It is used regularly by two departments at our school. ATI-Net offers weather reports from monitoring stations around California. Science teachers are using data from two of these weather monitoring stations in their class projects. They use the daily weather data to teach chart and graph-making skills. Three times a week the students are given the data for several weather parameters, and must translate that information into charts and graphs. I downloaded it for them twice a week during the spring semester.

The ATI-Net agriculture data includes both economic and political information on a large number of foreign countries in its Trade Library. This thorough information is gathered by the U.S. State Department. These are quite detailed reports and contain a lot of analytical data and comments made by experts in the host country. Our Economics teacher has his students use these reports as reference materials for their reports as part of a unit on Third World countries. The data is originally intended for the use of the California agribusiness community for use in their overseas trade planning. I download the data upon student request. Another very advanced database, World Bank Economic Data is now available, but may be a bit complex for the average student to master in time to include in their reports.

Another active user at Pleasant Valley High is one of our science teachers, who is also in charge of our International Baccalaureate Program. The I.B. Program is an international affiliation of secondary schools. They have set high standards of performance for students and expect much from their teachers. Their use of e-mail has greatly enhanced access to planning and curriculum information for our entire I.B. program, and has saved money in postal and fax expenses.

One area of our curriculum that I have been unable to get very involved is our English department. The Internet offers many excellent resources, such as Dartmouth's online Shakespeare database. But so far, I haven't been able to demonstrate it to many of our English teachers, or develop Internet-related curriculum with English teachers. I have shown various project announcements to some of them. Two have obtained CORE/Internet accounts, including our English chair. So little time . . .

I continue doing as much Internet "exploring" as possible, and have come across quite a few resources that appear useful. My goal is to involve as many teachers and classes as possible with the huge variety of resources that are available. My biggest concern is that most resources are still not very user-friendly at the present time. Most teachers cannot spare the time to become familiar with the quirks of each system or network, so we are moving ahead fairly slowly at this time. Perhaps this will always be the case. I am happy to be able to act as a reference librarian for our staff and students.

By the way, we currently have two Macintosh computers with modems and outside lines dedicated for student use, in addition to the modem connected to my Macintosh. All of our classrooms have telephone service, and a number of teachers have modems and computers in their classrooms. This winter we expect to add an ISDN option to both our PC-based CD-ROM computer and Macintosh networks in the library, with Gopher, Hytelnet, or other public domain software to allow them to connect directly with Internet resources.

I also use AskERIC and the ERIC Database to find information for various teachers and administrators who are looking for answers about innovations that we are contemplating. Pleasant Valley High is actively planning and experimenting with restructuring, and Internet resources such as discussion groups, AskERIC, and other K-12 sites have been extremely helpful to us.

I have been spending some time trying to develop a cadre of students in Internet searching, and have sponsored student accounts for them on CORE. I have aimed them toward various Campus-Wide Information Services (CWIS) sites, as well as Gopher and WorldWideWeb sites, which are resource-rich. The CWISs also have a very high interest profile for our students, as they have a lot of information about the host college or university, not to mention access to other useful informational databases.

It is an ongoing effort to get this group trained. The students are highly motivated, and enjoy helping each other, so it is not an area that I need to spend a lot of time. More than 100 of our students have CORE/Internet accounts, in addition to the teachers mentioned above. Some of them are my library aides. Others are students who have expressed an interest in what they see me doing regularly at my desk.

This is the third year that I have been in contact with our graduates via e-mail. I have set up a group folder on CORE with the e-addresses of our graduates. They are spread out across the country, and I am regularly exchanging news and information with one or another of them. I consider it a real treat to post one of their exciting messages to our staff bulletin board, and pass along greetings to individual teachers as the graduates ask me to do so. Many of our current students are also in touch through e-mail with their friends who are now in college.

Our library CD-ROM LAN is built around several key resources, TOM/Infotrac magazine index and full-text fiche collection; the SIRS Index with full-text; and Gale Research's DISCovering Authors. These are well-used and complement each other very well. We also provide DIALOG Database searching through the Classmate program, which is relatively inexpensive compared to their prime-time costs. I have not yet had a lot of success integrating Dialog into the curriculum, but have high hopes.

Working with the Internet has added an exciting and sophisticated aspect to the library media program and to our school's curriculum. It has given me an opportunity to work closely with many teachers and administrators in an area that provides them with instant rewards and positive recognition. It allows us to provide our students with the best possible access to information and human resources not normally available. It has allowed us to break down the isolation that many rural communities and most classroom teachers experience.

10

Library Media Specialists Move Center Stage
An Example of Implementation of Information Technologies

CAROL KROLL

Most school library media specialists share a common dream: they see their media centers acting as dynamic service centers that permeate every aspect of school life. They envision themselves as instructional leaders who work closely with other teachers to ensure the acquisition of information literacy and as key members of technology and curriculum planning teams that help design the future of information services in their districts.

In Nassau County, New York, this vision is fast becoming a reality. Through a long and deliberate process, school library media specialists have not only changed their own perceptions about their role and the mission of the library media center, but they have brought that vision to life in their school districts. Their accomplishments are giving schools state-of-the-art centers that are changing the nature of classroom assignments and assessments, generating new relationships with other teachers, and achieving respect from administrators and the school community at large. They have brought the school library to center stage.

Much of the change has been generated by the Nassau School Library System (NSLS) through its leadership development initiative and frequent workshops and programs. NSLS is one of 46 school library systems created by the New York State legislature in January 1985 under Commissioner's Regulations 90.18 of the Education Law. Library systems in New York State have a dual mission: 1) to serve their member libraries by enabling them to improve services to their users, and 2) to serve as components of the statewide library network, developing ways for all types of libraries to share resources through cooperation and coordination. To accomplish these missions, the NSLS provides educational and technical support to 56 school districts, including 328 public and private schools in Nassau County. The NSLS is supported by the state legislature via the Board of Cooperative Educational Services of Nassau County (Nassau BOCES), which acts as the fiscal agent and houses the System's offices.

113

STARTING THE CHANGE PROCESS

The changes set in motion by NSLS were not won easily or quickly. In 1986, a planning team of 35 library media specialists, two superintendents, and the director of NSLS met with Dr. Kenneth Tewel, a Queens College professor, to discuss the state of library services. There was an explosion of discontent by media specialists lamenting their poor working conditions. A needs assessment had identified the same general feeling of dissatisfaction with the lack of regard for media specialists and the absence of training at the school site.

The planning team decided that the school library media specialists would need to reframe their vision to themselves before a change in function could take place. The objective was no less than to ensure that media specialists could—and would—function as full-fledged faculty members and become part of the school's leadership team.

As a first step, a group was appointed to research the current thinking of school library media leaders. After reflection and much discussion, the planning team decided to create a new type of staff development program and peer support network. They embarked on an initiative to change the role and image of the school library media specialists.

The initiative was named Networks Enriching Teaching (NET) and the team hired Dr. Tewel to train media specialists to serve as facilitators. The idea was to establish regional clusters for mutual support. The facilitators would help cluster members; plan meeting content; create a warm, welcoming environment within each cluster; encourage participation in the initiative; and support an ongoing commitment to upgrade library services. Facilitators would continue to receive training in both group process and educational pedagogy, and would serve as library mentors for the county.

The facilitator leadership training that was implemented includes 1) understanding the life cycle of groups, 2) creating healthy groups focused on mature decision making, 3) giving and receiving feedback, and 4) dealing with conflict. After seven years, close to 50 facilitators have been trained and more than 150 library media specialists have become involved. Facilitators report increased ability to focus on the concerns of the group, more reflective exchanges, less posturing, and increased participation by group members. Leadership skills used with NET groups are easily transferred to interactions with students and fellow teachers. Led by the trained facilitators, groups meet every six weeks, after school, to share frustrations and problems, discuss possible solutions, and describe exemplary services. The facilitators continue to receive training, with new media specialists joining the group and others leaving after a two- or three-year stint.

Some outcomes of the initiative occurred as anticipated, others emerged as by-products. In addition to the specific accomplishments described in this article, a sure sign of success is the marked increase in support by district superintendents for school library media specialists. Further, in 1988, NSLS won the AASL/ABC-CLIO Leadership Development Award.

The NET initiative is the backbone of all that its members do. Each summer, a day is spent evaluating NET and planning for the next year. In response to members' suggestions, NSLS publishes a newsletter to share current ideas from the library and education fields, descriptions of exemplary media programs, bibliographies, discussion from NET group meetings, and calendar events. NET group members identify potential workshops, and speakers are hired to teach requested courses.

PRACTICAL ACCOMPLISHMENTS

The introduction of state-of-the-art technology to the NSLS has had a dramatic impact on the library media specialist's role and the media center's relationship to teaching. Library media specialists teach the use of the online catalog and circulation system, CD-ROMs, online databases, and the Internet to broaden information resources available to teachers and students. They work with principals and classroom teachers to change the nature of research assignments and the assessment process. As examples are the following:

Manhasset Junior High School

Media specialist Judy Taylor reports that, in one class period, students can now have access to a wealth of material not even available before. Additionally, many students have Prodigy at home and can print out encyclopedia entries and glue and paste them. As a result, teachers are developing new kinds of assignments that go beyond simple reporting. Recently, at Taylor's middle school, seventh-graders had to research wetlands issues and then hold a debate. After doing the research, they had to really think the subject through, so they could discuss it. They were able to obtain current relevant information from local government records as well as from questions answered by specialists, both located through e-mail on the Internet.

Great Neck High School

Media specialist Julia Van de Water has discovered that, in working with students, research is "not just a matter of physical access to materials, but of intellectual access as well—that is, judging the authority of the author and the timeliness of the material."

Bethpage High School

Media specialist Claire Donohue reports on the evolution of the research process this way:

> Students can now do incredible things. Our economics classes have long had to research a corporation—follow its stock, analyze its history and its prospects. In the beginning, we could only give them the daily paper to follow the stock market. Then, we found some affordable business reference tools. Next, we added online access to business databases, then a CD-ROM periodical index. Now, the Securities and Exchange Commission (SEC) is publishing annual reports on the Internet.

> An assignment that once called for great ingenuity, a lot of time in the public library, and/or a well-placed mentor, can now be completed in a fraction of the time in the school library. We have to change our ideas of what constitutes research and work with classroom and subject area teachers to design academically rigorous long-range assignments that acquaint students with sophisticated problem-solving strategies.

REAPING THE BENEFITS
OF AUTOMATION

Another key issue for school libraries is automation. There is a growing gap between libraries that are automated and those that are not. The NSLS is instrumental in making school library automation practical in Nassau County.

Each year, in partnership with the Long Island School Media Association, NSLS offers between 10 and 15 technology workshops for library media specialists. Programs might include instruction on Hypermedia, cataloging audiovisual equipment, uses of fiber optics in the school, connecting CD hardware, educational implications of use of the Internet, or grant writing. During the summer of 1993-94, participants in a well-attended, week-long course taught by Pam Berger, library media specialist at Byram Hills (New York) High School, learned how to effectively use CD-ROM as part of their instructional programs. Also, NSLS has given grants of fax machines and CD hardware to schools without them.

NSLS further supports the county's school libraries in a New York State program called "Electronic Doorway Libraries." Libraries that qualify receive statewide recognition. To qualify, a library must use technology to enhance information retrieval and resource sharing, with a flow of requests and information both into and out of a library by electronic means. Libraries must have catalog records that have been converted into machine readable format, provide access to at least one other database located outside the library, have computer equipment, use technology to provide quality library services, participate in state-approved automation and resource sharing programs, and work with its library system in making full use of present and future technologies. A tall order to accomplish—made easier if the library media specialist can turn to a school library system for help.

One way the Nassau School Library System brings automation to the school library media center is by establishing a union catalog of the resources in each participating school library. Each year, members send 400-800 catalog shelflist cards to NSLS where they are converted into a machine readable format. These titles form the NSLS union catalog that is housed at the NSLS office. Districts access the 350,000 titles in the union catalog via a modem, and leave an interlibrary loan request for the desired resources. Delivery vans support the service. As each school installs its own online catalog and circulation system, titles already converted for the NSLS union catalog are given to the school to be merged with the rest of the school's holdings. The school, in turn, adds its newly converted titles to the NSLS union catalog.

To avoid costly mistakes and to encourage resource sharing, New York State offers financial aid to districts that automate through a school library system. NSLS has designed configurations for the hardware and software that districts need for an online catalog and circulation system with modem access to the NSLS union catalog. NSLS staff members meet with district and school-level administrators and media specialists to plan for the automation process. These planning discussions are usually lengthy and center on educational implications.

Nassau School Library System members have selected the purchase of Mandarin, an online catalog and circulation system that supports multiple databases. As a result, members can add a wide range of data to their online catalog and circulation systems including whole language classroom collections, schoolwide CD-ROM collections, and district audiovisual equipment.

School library media specialists can easily evaluate their automated collection to determine subject strengths and gaps. Instead of each school building having a separate collection, districtwide collections can be developed. Plans have begun for district and countywide coordinated collection purchasing.

At the NSLS office, Mandarin is used to manage multiple databases. NSLS has become a model pilot site for a partnership between Media Flex, Inc., the distributor of Manadarin, and EBSCO, Inc. EBSCO has mounted its magazine service onto the NSLS Mandarin online catalog software. Students can dial into the NSLS union catalog, choose "EBSCO" from the menu, and view 270 magazine titles. They use the same strategy to locate a magazine article as they would to search for a book title.

To further enhance use of the union catalog, NSLS staff, with the assistance of Media Flex, is now evaluating mounting the union catalog on the Internet. This would enable unlimited access to the union catalog by the whole school community—from home or school—with either an IBM or Apple computer. Some district administrators voice concern about making their holdings available to anyone browsing the Internet. There are ethical and legal questions to be explored.

The new technology that has been incorporated into the media centers offers the districts other broad benefits. Some districts are wiring their schools and exploring possibilities for access to electronic information sources including the Internet, CD-ROMs, and the online catalog from classrooms, school administrative and department offices, and students' homes. Senior citizens can become active members of the school library's resources without leaving their homes—a valuable community relations asset for many districts.

NSLS also offers library media specialists a password to the Internet, and training in its use, as a result of a partnership formed with Long Island-based Hofstra University. NSLS is arranging to install telephone lines and modems at the Hofstra Internet site to enable all school library media centers to gain Internet access. Hofstra University is also interested in fostering support of the K-12 community by creating a mentoring program to connect science and math professors with the K-12 community.

In many ways, NSLS is providing a mechanism to free media centers of limitations imposed by walls and doors, by bringing in human and electronic resources from the community and the world beyond.

KEEPING MEMBERS UP TO DATE

Members of NSLS are encouraged to read current articles and books written by leading thinkers in their field: education. Bibliographies are distributed and attention is directed to particular authors including Ted Sizer, Linda Darling-Hammond, Howard Gardner, Lauren Resnick, Susan Fuhrman, Rexford Brown, and James Comer. Recent talks to NSLS members have included information about authentic assessment, cooperative learning, inclusion, "untracking," multiculturalism, and constructivism.

In order to interact with other teachers as equals, library media specialists must also understand statewide initiatives, mandates, and national trends. Two November 1993 documents, "Learning-Centered Curriculum and Assessment for New York State," and "Reports of the Curriculum and Assessment Committees" (produced by the New York State Curriculum and Assessment Council to the Commissioner of

Education and the Board of Regents), were distributed to a representative of each school district. Media specialists were urged to approach their principals with the request that they serve as schoolwide trainers and interpreters of the documents. The new role for media specialists will position them as agents of change.

Some of the finest thinkers in school librarianship have worked with NSLS members. In 1986, Inabeth Miller, at that time director of the Boston Science Museum (now director of the Massachusetts Corporation for Educational Telecommunications [MCET]), talked about her start as a school library specialist in a library located in a coal bin. She inspired NSLS members to achieve what is possible. They have since stayed in contact with her; when MCET won a Federal Star Schools Projects Grant, she arranged for two NSLS members to be recipients.

Carol Kuhlthau, Associate Professor, Rutgers School of Communication, Information and Library Studies, presented her research on the Information Search Process, in which the library media specialist, the subject-area teacher, and the student interact through intensive, long-term research projects. This approach has become widely accepted throughout the country.

Because working collaboratively with subject-area teachers is central to the information search process, we invited Carol-Ann Page, President of The Human Resources Development Group, to help NSLS members more fully understand media specialist/teacher partnerships. Jacqueline Mancall, Professor at Drexel University College of Information Studies, expanded their understanding of online searching and the uses of databases in the instructional program. Mike Eisenberg, Professor at Syracuse University's School of Information Studies, a major influence on our actions, spent a day energizing administrators to support their library media centers and to move them into the twenty-first century.

Throughout the years, each speaker's presentation has been followed by a full-day workshop and much discussion. The work of each speaker built upon the previous ideas that had been offered. When NSLS members were ready to act on all they had heard and articulate a definition of their own vision, they asked Shirley Aaron, Professor at Florida State University's School of Library and Information Studies, to join them. Her provocative questions and uncanny ability to pull multiple ideas together provided the impetus to move ahead.

WHAT'S NEXT FOR NSLS MEMBERS?

Eleven individuals interested in discussing ideas for the future of countywide information services have formed a committee named "The Optimists." Members include a superintendent, two assistant superintendents for curriculum, an elementary principal, four library media specialists, and the director of NSLS. Members will explore, together, what is to come next and decide how their aims can be achieved.

This ongoing process of change is both invigorating and challenging. The goal is clear—to provide outstanding services to students and teachers. NSLS members have come a long way toward achieving that goal. The beauty of it is that there is no limit to what a group of library media specialists can accomplish.

11
Networking Schools in Wisconsin

NEAH J. LOHR

INTRODUCTION TO WISCONSIN

Wisconsin currently has 427 school districts with slightly more than 2,000 school buildings located in rural, suburban, and urban areas of the state. These districts range in size from fewer than 300 students to more than 95,000 students in PK-12. There are 12 regional Cooperative Education Service Agencies (CESAs), with every school district being a geographical part of one CESA. The CESAs offer a variety of services to the districts within their boundaries, depending upon the needs and the contracting of these services by the districts. The districts are governed locally and are therefore autonomous.

WISCONSIN'S NETWORKING OPTIONS

Over the past several years, there have been several attempts to connect Wisconsin's school districts, public libraries, CESAs, government, and higher education for communication, collaboration, and access to online resources, including the Internet.

Wisenet

WiseNet (*Wisconsin Education Network*) is Wisconsin's comprehensive telecommunications system, which was developed and is maintained by the Wisconsin Department of Public Instruction. WiseNet transmits educational information around the clock to any location in Wisconsin. Educational institutions in the state can access Wisenet through a toll-free number, with a minimal investment of time and money. The WiseNet Bulletin Board System is a service provided to school districts and CESAs that gives quick and easy access to information from around the state and nation, bypassing the traditional system of printing and mailing. The system features an electronic mail system, educational news section, special interest group board, and an upload and download file section.

Advantages of using WiseNet include:

- Saving on postage expenses by using e-mail
- Saving on long-distance phone calls
- Able to post or read meeting agendas, minutes, and workshop and training announcements
- Able to share information and ideas quickly with other professionals
- Able to send announcements to a statewide or regional audience
- Able to file annual reports and budget reports at any time

Learning Link Wisconsin

Another fast, easy, and free online computer service for Wisconsin K-12 educators is Learning Link Wisconsin, provided by the Wisconsin Educational Communications Board. Learning Link Wisconsin features a section called "Curriculum Connection," forums, and electronic mail.

Learning Link Wisconsin provides free, round the clock online computer service and the ability to

- Expedite curriculum development
- Enhance classroom lessons
- Learn of professional development opportunities
- Discover the resources available from educational facilities and organizations
- Communicate with colleagues throughout the state

It also offers users a connection to the Internet for e-mail. But the unique feature of Learning Link is Curriculum Connection. This allows coordination of instructional television programming with curriculum development and classroom lessons.

WISCNet

In early spring, 1991, the higher education data network, WISCNet, became operational. This network consists of all 26 institutions of the University of Wisconsin System and eight private colleges and universities in Wisconsin. WISCNet was formed and partially funded over a three-year period through National Science Foundation (NSF) support in the form of a $589,000 grant. This network supports access to the CICNet, NSFNet, and national computational resources and databases and provides communication among researchers and teachers, including access to the Internet.

While the Department of Public Instruction recognized the importance of computer electronic communications, the high costs of access to WISCNet were prohibitive to the K-12 school districts. Budgetary constraints, in school districts, at the regional level, and at the state level prevented a statewide initiative for connectivity.

Some of the institutions of higher education have been allowing nearby school districts access through the campus connections. The costs for this backdoor, dial-up access have ranged from nothing to more than $2,000 annually. With the increased use of the network, the need for more bandwidth and more support has resulted in some change beginning in July 1994. All of the school districts will have to pay a fee and some districts will have to establish a full account at the local college or university to have access to WISCNet. Another problem for K-12 schools is that many are not geographically located near a college campus, so connectivity is nearly impossible due to the high cost of toll charges and distance.

INTERNET ACCESS POLICY STATEMENT AND PLAN

The Wisconsin Department of Public Instruction (DPI), Division for Libraries and Community Learning developed an Internet Access Policy Statement and Plan, which has now been adopted as the DPI plan.

The Policy Statement is as follows:

The Internet is a major component of the evolving National Information Infrastructure (NII), which is commonly referred to as the "Information Superhighway." Access to this expanding information network has the potential to dramatically change the way schools and libraries operate and significantly increase access to the information and knowledge resources which Wisconsin residents need to achieve personal and further societal goals. Educational and library institutions should play a leadership role in facilitating this access and in making use of the Internet to carry out their missions. The Department of Public Instruction is committed to working with the state government, the federal government, telecommunications vendors, and library and educational institutions at all levels to ensure that Wisconsin residents benefit to the greatest extent possible by this new and promising technology.

The goals are

- By the year 2000 every educational and library organization in Wisconsin will have full, dedicated (not dial-up) access to the Internet.

- By the year 2000 every Wisconsin resident will have access to the Internet through a toll-free telephone call.

The ability to meet these goals will be influenced by a host of factors including fiscal and technical constraints and the knowledge base and staffing needed for network administration and use at the local level.

The objectives to meet these goals are

1. To promote and facilitate use of the Internet by schools and libraries to carry out their missions.

2. To promote and facilitate use of the Internet for sharing information resources among all types of libraries.

3. To promote and facilitate use of the Internet by providing information resources to the education and library communities and the public from the DPI and other state agencies.

4. To promote and facilitate use of the Internet for employees of the Department of Public Instruction and other state agencies.

5. To use the Internet to carry out departmental and division programs and services.

The Internet Access Policy Statement and Plan will be carried out by the DPI's Internet Work Groups, in coordination and cooperation with other state agencies and the state's education and library communities.

THE STATUS OF WISCONSIN'S NETWORKING PLAN

To further the vision, outlined in the Internet Access Policy Statement and Plan, several efforts are currently in progress. Through the use of an Ameritech grant, all state agencies now have newly installed direct nodes to provide access to the Internet. The Department of Administration (DOA) has recently established a state gopher, called "Badger," The Wisconsin State Agency Internet Gopher. The Department of Public Instruction has been working with DOA and now is contributing information to the gopher. Electronic links from the DPI menu have been made to gophers at the United States Department of Education, other state education agencies, ERIC, the Library of Congress and the American Library Association. The Badger gopher can be accessed with a gopher client or by Telnet.

As of spring 1995, the Department of Administration's "lottery line" is available for statewide access by educators to the Internet using a SLIP connection. This Wisconsin Internet Access Program will be called "Badger Dial." This will provide a basic level of Internet access throughout the state at a reasonable cost to all public sector agencies. The Department of Public Instruction's Division for Libraries and Community Learning staff will be involved in training new public school and public library users on the use of this connection.

THE FUTURE OF WISCONSIN'S NETWORKING PLANS

There are ongoing discussions and plans among key personnel in the various state agencies as to how best to link all school buildings (more than 2,000) in the 426 districts and all public libraries (380), as well as governmental units and eventually homes. Agencies involved at the present time are: the Governor's agency, Department of Administration; Department of Public Instruction; University of Wisconsin Systems, Division of Information Technology; and the University of

Wisconsin-Extension, the Education Communications Board, Department of Natural Resources, and the Vocational Technical College System.

The state of Wisconsin operates under a biennial budget. Recent direction from the Department of Administration to all state agencies is to present budget initiatives that will maintain the status quo but reflect a 5 percent or 10 percent budget cut. It is very difficult to acquire any technology or related initiatives without actually increasing the budget. So, the Department of Public Instruction's state superintendent is proposing reallocation of some of the current funding.

One of the budget initiatives that I am directly involved with is that of Instructional Technology and Staff Development. Through a reallocation of staff development dollars, we are proposing that an additional 20 nodes for direct Internet connections be funded and developed throughout the state. These nodes would be located in the Cooperative Education Service Agency offices (12) and/or the Public Library System headquarters/Resources Library offices (17). Where these offices are located in the same city or proximity, there would be only one node. These agencies will need to submit a plan of operation and outreach that will include expansion, implementation, support, staff development, and continuation of the network, both within their buildings and to the local education agencies and public libraries in their service areas.

Wisconsin Telco Bill

On July 5, 1994, the Governor of Wisconsin, Tommy Thompson, signed "1993 Wisconsin Act 496" relating to the deregulation of the telecommunications industry that became law on September 1, 1994. The legislation was enacted to implement some of the recommendations of the Governor's Blue Ribbon Telecommunications Infrastructure Task Force. The basic purpose of the legislation is to establish a new regulatory model for telecommunications utilities to reflect the transition to a competitive telecommunications marketplace. This is a very complex law with some of the implementation process still to be completed.

Highlights include:

- The Public Service Commission (PSC) is directed to regulate telecommunications utilities with the goal of developing alternative forms of regulation other than the rate-of-return. The "incentive regulation" is to promote competition, infrastructure deployment, economic development, consumer choice, productivity, efficiency, quality of life, societal goals, and universal service.

- An immediate 10% rate reduction for Ameritech residential and small business access lines. Local residential service, standard business, and small business usage rates must be frozen for three years. Annual price increases may be deferred for a maximum of three years into a single increase, but limited to 10% or the increase in the gross domestic product price index, whichever is greater. A telecom utility may only file one rate increase during any 12-month period.

- A Universal Service Fund is established to ensure affordable service to low-income customers and rural and high-cost areas of the state. On January 1, 1996, telecommunications providers must contribute to the fund in proportion to their gross operating revenues from intrastate telecommunications services.

- Many consumer protections are included in the law. For example, billing for services not ordered and disconnection of local service for failure to pay for optional services are prohibited as is the charge for local service based on duration or time of day a call is made. Privacy protections are also included in the new law.

- An Advanced Telecommunications Foundation is established to fund technology projects and educate consumers about advanced services. Priority will be given to projects in school districts where the expenditures per student are below state average spending levels. This includes a "Fast Start" provision of $5 million targeted for technical applications in the schools. The foundation will have a fund of over $40 million, with the state contributing $500,000 and the balance from private industry.

- Creation of a telecommunications retraining board to determine how retraining funds should be expended for displaced telecommunications workers. This board will have seven members to include three members representing unions of members in the telecommunications industry, three members representing telecom companies, and one member that is from the technical college system board.

As a direct result of deregulation, Ameritech has committed to bringing fiber optics to all of the high schools and junior high/middle schools in its territory throughout the state, along with a 'just in time' service for elementary schools that are ready to use fiber optics. Ameritech will invest at least $700 million in new equipment and technology during the next five years. They will expand the fiber optic connections to include colleges, universities, vocational schools, and major public libraries in Ameritech territory. The General Telephone Company is in the process of filing its intentions with the PSC. Wisconsin is beginning to see an expanding list of established and new start-up providers of networking services.

At the Wisconsin Department of Public Instruction, there is an overall DPI Internet committee, an Internal Internet committee, and an External Internet committee. All of these are researching and planning the best way to connect all of the internal DPI employees and external school buildings for equal affordable access to the Internet.

Wisconsin is also a Goals 2000: Educate America Act state and has received approval and funding for restructuring education under this law. Grants will be made to school districts that qualify through an application process now in place. A statewide technology task force will be named to develop a state technology plan, which will include Internet access for all PK-12 students as well as faculty and administrators. With all of this activity, Wisconsin should have some interesting developments in the area of statewide connectivity.

BIBLIOGRAPHY

Bocher, Robert. *Frequently Asked Questions (FAQ) on Badger Dial: A Wisconsin Dial Internet Access Program.* A State Department of Administration, Department of Public Instruction, WISCNet and Ameritech Cooperative Statewide Dial Internet program. 1995.

1993 Wisconsin Act 496 (The New Wisconsin Telecommunications Act).

Wisconsin Advanced Telecommunications Foundation, 93-94 Wis. Stats. Sec.14.28.

Wisconsin Department of Public Instruction. *Wisenet: Wisconsin Education Network* Bulletin Board System. Brochure. 1994.

Wisconsin ECB. *Link Up! to Learning Link Wisconsin.* Brochure. n.d.

Part IV

Education for Library Media Specialists

12

School Library Media Specialist as Knowledge Navigator
Preparing for the Electronic Environment

ᘒ **KATHLEEN BURNETT and MARY JANE McNALLY** ᘍ

INTRODUCTION

Imagine visiting a public elementary school, middle school, and high school. As you pass the media center, you pause to observe the activity:

Elementary School
Next week is Martin Luther King, Jr. Day. Two fourth-graders return to the library to prepare a class presentation. They have already read the biography assigned in class. Each sits down at one of the diverse multimedia workstations. They outline their presentation, passing information back and forth instantaneously. First, they outline Martin Luther King, Jr.'s life. As they work, they access the various picture resources available on CD-ROM on the local area network. They work cooperatively, one child finding the pictures, the other cutting and pasting them into the outline. They decide that they want to focus on King's "I Have a Dream" speech. One searches the local resources while the other uses a Mosaic client to search for video footage of the speech on the Internet. Within five minutes, the second child has located a QuickTime movie of the event in a public database. He downloads it to the computer he is working on, and pastes it into the "report." The first child joins the second, and they play back the movie several times, discussing the segments that they find most interesting as they watch. The first child returns to his workstation and connects to the library catalog. He finds three books listed that he thinks might include some analysis of the speech. He heads over to the book stacks to retrieve them. The second child edits the movie footage, breaking it into segments for analysis. The first child returns with two books and hands one to his partner. They read quietly for awhile until one pipes up: "Listen to this!" The two children proceed to record their own analyses of the speech, taking turns with the microphone. Now and then they quote the authors of the books. When they have finished, they play back the entire presentation, write a conclusion, and attach a bibliography that includes citations for all the resources they have used, both print and electronic.

129

Middle School

A dyslexic middle school student has to prepare a report on the novel she has recently completed. She has worked very hard and has read the book completely on her own, but she is overwhelmed by the prospect of preparing the report, which is due next week. Since her dyslexia makes it difficult for her to express herself in writing, the teacher has suggested that she prepare a multimedia presentation, which she can then share with the class. She enters the library media center and sits down at one of the multimedia workstations. The iconic user interface facilitates her movement through the various resources available. After browsing through files of appropriate images, she decides that what she would like to do is "illustrate" the novel. She records her voice as she retells the story. Then, using a multimedia authoring program, she intersperses the pictures she has found to illustrate the various scenes. When she cannot find an appropriate picture resource, she moves to a drawing program and creates her own, then pastes it into her presentation. The presentation has taken her less time than she had expected. There are still two days left until it is due. She decides to add short written captions for each picture.

High School

A high school science teacher enters the library. She has come to consult with the library media specialist. Recently, these two convinced the school board to purchase hardware and software that support a virtual reality physics laboratory. Although the equipment was relatively expensive, the board had agreed to the placement of an additional workstation in the existing school media library facilities so that students would have access to laboratory equipment outside scheduled lab times. As they talk, the science teacher learns from the library media specialist that the workstation is one of the most heavily used resources in the collection. She is not surprised to hear this. The impact on the physics classes has been enormous. Although the school year is only slightly more than half over, her students have already mastered the material in her lesson plans from the previous year! She has come in hopes that the library media specialist may be able to recommend supplementary materials to support further exploration.

Science fiction? Utopian futurism? No. The scenarios above illustrate some of the many ways in which three emerging technologies—multimedia, networking, and virtual reality—might be deployed in education within the next five to ten years. The location of these technologies in the library media center is deliberate but not inevitable. Multimedia, networking, and virtual reality will be important components of the information infrastructure of the future, just as traditional resources, such as print and audiovisual materials, and more recent additions, such as textual CD-ROM and online databases, are important components today. The emerging technologies will more likely accelerate the evolutionary process that library media centers have been experiencing since the introduction of nonprint media in the sixties than they will bring it to an end. While the metamorphosis from the "school library" to the "library media center" was by no means a trivial one, the potential for fundamental transformation is much greater now, if only because successful integration of the emerging technologies will be fostered by the adoption of new interaction models.

These new models present opportunities and challenges to the library media specialist. In an environment increasingly evolving toward connection and integration, the library media specialist's role must change. Gone are the days when the media specialist's responsibilities were defined by the four walls of the institution's library and the size of its print collection. Today, library media specialists are expected to be experts in the use of all types of media. Tomorrow, their expertise will need to extend to the integration and production of multimedia in digital form. They will have to become information designers as well as information managers. Today, the responsibilities of the library media specialist are no longer strictly bound by the four walls of the library. With the introduction of online databases to the library media center, the first tendrils of connection to the vast world of information beyond the institution's walls were formed. These tendrils will continue to grow, and the library media specialist must grow with them. Today's library media specialist is an expert pathfinder. Tomorrow's library media specialist will be a knowledge navigator.

ACTION AGENDA

This discussion proposes an action agenda that will move the library media center from a locus of isolation to one of connection, from a print to a digital library. The adoption of such an agenda will initiate a new approach to information literacy and the role that information seeking plays in education, and will, consequently, radically alter the function of the library media center vis-à-vis the institution and its community. Currently, we are witnessing the emergence of global communities interconnected through telecommunications networks; soon we will witness an evolution of the library media center, from an information consumer to an information contributor.

The action agenda consists of four phases:

1. Defining new models of information processing and developing curricula based on these models;

2. Short-range educational planning and coordination for the adoption of the models and curricula;

3. Training and education of library media specialists and library media specialist candidates in the models and the technological innovations; and

4. Long-range educational planning and curriculum revision.

Defining Models and Developing Curricula

Models of the process of information seeking that acknowledge evolving theories of communication, collaboration, and multiple intelligences and recognize the increasing importance of technological innovation are being developed (Belkin 1980; Kuhlthau 1993). Source-based information search models are too limited to encompass the range of possibilities that emerging technologies present. Successful models need to emphasize flexibility and adaptiveness in the understanding of learners, the tools they use, and the environments in which they learn. They must also incorporate the full range of information-processing activities. Recent cognitive models of the information search process in K-12 education (Eisenberg and Berkowitz 1990) and the information retrieval processes of adults (Belkin 1980) provide excellent examples of process models that might be adapted. In *Seeking Meaning*, Kuhlthau provides a solid theoretical foundation and a process model of information seeking (1993). Though this model was developed and tested in traditional library settings with little or no technological components, its emphasis on information seeking as individualized process learning and its recognition of affective as well as cognitive aspects of this process, make it flexible and adaptable to a high-technology environment.

Applying Multiple Intelligences Theory

Traditional thinking defines intelligence as a single quality measured by an IQ score. Gardner, dissatisfied with the prevailing view, has posed a theory of multiple intelligences; loosely associated primarily independent abilities. Specifically, Gardner's theory enumerates the following seven forms of intelligence: linguistic, musical, logical-mathematical, spatial, bodily-kinesthetic, interpersonal, and intrapersonal. The cluster of abilities comprising each of these intelligences can be used as a means of acquiring information. In contrast to the traditional view, the theory of multiple intelligences seeks to underscore the fact that the ways of knowing are present in virtually every realm of human activity (1983).

As computers and interactive multimedia proliferate in classrooms and library media centers, they will help teachers and students acquire and synthesize information in ways compatible with various intelligences. Computers and interactive media require students to be active participants, not passive observers. Because of the tactile nature of computer inputs—keyboard, mouse, touch screen—and the critical requirement of eye-hand coordination, computers contribute to kinesthetic learning. Computer simulations, which enhance the feeling of being within a given environment or context, also amplify aspects of kinesthetic learning.

Spatial learning is encouraged through the use of hypertextual technologies, including such familiar programs as HyperCard and interactive videodisc and CD-ROM to locate information and create traditional reports. Involving students in the hypertext and multimedia authoring processes can further enhance spatial learning. Students may create interactive multimedia experiences that can be shared with their classmates as well as the teacher. An extreme example of spatial visual technology is virtual reality. Here the student must act completely with the structure of the virtual situation. Textual multi-user environments currently available through the Internet, such as MOOs (multi-user object oriented) and MUDs (multi-user dungeons), offer an intermediate step toward this kind of spatial emersion. These textual environments, many of which are based on popular fantasy and science fiction books available in the school media center, are structured around architectural and spatial principles.

Computers and multimedia devices are tools that students can use successfully in groups. Such collaborative experiences help students enhance their interpersonal learning and develop interpersonal communication skills. By providing yet another connection, networks such as KidsNet and Learning Network help students to extend interpersonal skills from face-to-face to mediated modes of communication. Students who are resistant to the formality of letter-writing necessary in traditional pen-pal arrangements often enjoy the less formal environment that e-mail fosters. The introduction of video conferencing software may eventually make it possible for students in the United States to communicate audiovisually with students as far away as Great Britain or Australia.

As should be clear from these examples, the use of multiple modalities helps foster holistic thinking. It also allows students to build and be more aware of the mental models they employ while searching for, analyzing, evaluating, and using information.

Using Communication Theory

Many library media centers have already made the first steps toward incorporating communication technologies, such as local area networks, community bulletin boards, and connectivity to either commercial networks (e.g., Prodigy, Connect, CompuServe) or the Internet. Currently, these technologies are being used to support fairly traditional, largely print-based information seeking by students.

Most print-based information-seeking models assume a relative stability of documents at both the individual and the collection level. As new items are added to the collection, new surrogates are created for them. The surrogates include pointers to the documents, which are intended to facilitate their retrieval. In a print-based system, acquisition of new items and the creation of surrogates are expensive, labor-intensive processes. The economics of the situation thus contributes to its stability. It is worthwhile to invest in new documents and to provide good surrogates for them because the documents themselves will remain unchanged, and their relation to the collection as a whole will show little variability over time. Those parts of the collection that do show frequent variability, such as periodical collections, have traditionally been provided for by externally produced indexes, such as the *Readers' Guide to Periodical Literature*. Originally issued in paper form, these indexes are currently also available in online and CD-ROM form.

A networked environment strains the print-based model in four ways: 1) much of the "information" available on the networks does not exist in document form in the traditional sense—participants in discussion-group conversations, for example, tend to think of their communications as more closely related to telephone conversations than unpublished documents; 2) conversely, because anyone with an account can participate in discussion-group conversations, and because a public, written record of that communication is created, students might be expected to repeatedly experience a phenomenon akin to print publication; 3) even when information retrieved from network servers does exist in the form of a document, the ease with which the document can be revised—without the knowledge or permission of the original author—undermines the document's integrity; and 4) the boundaries of the local collection no longer limit individual transactions because information searching and information delivery are more frequently conducted outside those boundaries.

A curriculum designed around source-based information search strategies is bound to fail, not only because it requires increasingly frequent modification to reflect new sources and technologies, but also because it appears highly unlikely that any technology will exhibit the primacy that print once held. As the information search process becomes less print-bound, it will also become less document oriented. A successful model of the information search process will therefore have as its focus an understanding of information searching as a constructive process. The Information Search Process (ISP) model (Kuhlthau 1993), which incorporates cognitive and affective human information behavior, provides a cohesive framework for information retrieval in a networked multimedia environment while allowing for individuation of the search process. This model may be easily extended to encompass information-processing learning in its entirety.

One of the most exciting potentials of the network environment is the development of new paradigms for information searching, retrieval, and delivery. Developing standards for machine interoperability should facilitate the design of customized human-computer interfaces, which will decrease the need for individuals to learn multiple search protocols while it simultaneously supports individualized information search processes. Students' learning can therefore be more effectively focused on understanding the cognitive and affective aspects of their own information search behaviors, rather than on the mechanics of interacting with diverse machines.

The primary shortcoming of most process-based models is that they tend to isolate the process of information seeking from other information-processing activities. Interactive communications technologies, such as multimedia and networked communication, provide excellent opportunities to break out of this isolation. The costs of computer-mediated communication are dropping so precipitously that it is not unrealistic for schools to set up network servers that can serve as "publisher's clearinghouses" for student work. Both the costs and usability of multimedia hardware and software are approaching levels where schools can realistically consider adding facilities to classrooms. Models limited to a single aspect of the information process—the search process—made sense in the collection-bound environment of the library media centers of the past, but these models will not provide an adequate basis for understanding the information-processing learning that will take place in the integrated and connected library media center of the near future. We need to begin seriously reexamining the human-computer and human-human interaction models that provide the foundation for much of what we do in education.

Introducing Collaboration into the
Library Media Center Environment

Traditional library structures were predisposed to support the individual information-gathering and quiet, individual study that earlier educational philosophies fostered and encouraged. Reading silently was encouraged; reading aloud, discouraged. Exercises were designed to help individuals complete individual assignments individually, something that most print resources, which are difficult to share simultaneously, support quite efficiently. The introduction of audiovisual materials, especially in centers where playback equipment was available on-site, supported a concurrent evolution in classroom curricula toward an environment that fosters cooperative learning and collaboration. This evolution is being continued with the introduction of computers into the library media center, and will be extended by the introduction of multimedia, networking, and virtual reality technologies in particular.

Students pursuing school media certification in the MLS program at Rutgers University are required to take a course titled "Multimedia Structure, Organization, Access and Production" as well as courses in curriculum design, learning theory, and readers' response-approach to materials. The first time the course was offered (spring 1992), a collaborative project was required largely because sufficient equipment was not available to support individual projects. What was learned in that first semester, however, has led not only to a continuing requirement that students work in the collaborative mode, but to extending consideration of collaborative learning to the design of the multimedia presentations required in partial satisfaction of the course requirements.

Virtual reality and multimedia (especially when hypertextual capabilities are included) can be deployed effectively as learning tools to support: 1) classroom teaching, 2) individual exploration and reinforcement, and 3) both classroom and independent collaborative learning. Early multimedia design, which involved elaborate workstation setups including laserdisc players, focused on the support of classroom teaching, using hypertextual linking to facilitate the teacher's ability to move quickly from one part of the presentation to another, to replay portions, and to focus on those aspects of particular interest. The publishers of many of these early productions have advocated supplemental individual student use for reinforcement purposes, but the cost of the elaborate workstations has tended to mitigate any such implementation. More recent productions, which rely on fully digitized multimedia and therefore require little in the way of peripheral equipment for playback, appear to be focusing on individual exploration and reinforcement. It is interesting to note, however, that library media specialists from across the country report that it is a rare occurrence when an individual student uses any multimedia software in isolation. This extends even to multimedia encyclopedias on CD-ROM. Intentionally designing collaborative support into multimedia courseware will only further this process.

The introduction of multimedia software for student authoring holds even greater potential in the creation of collaborative learning environments (Hamm and Adams 1992). Successful multimedia authoring requires a spectrum of skills and abilities of which traditional textual authoring is a single element. The incorporation of visual and audio acuity; organizational logic; design; editing; and information searching, processing, and evaluation skills into both the learning and assessment processes can be facilitated. As with textual authoring, students will exhibit different skill levels in each area at different developmental stages, and most students will exhibit consistent strengths and weaknesses across stages. A supportive, collaborative environment can help students to identify and strengthen their weaknesses and to build upon their strengths through interaction with their peers.

Though collaboration can take place almost anywhere, using almost any tool, a well-designed and well-thought-out physical environment, including computer hardware and software designed to facilitate rather than hinder collaboration, is crucial to the successful incorporation of collaboration in the learning process (Harel and Papert 1991; Hamm and Adams 1992). The physical layout of the environment, the technology that supports it, and day-to-day adult supervision are areas that the library media specialist of the near future will be called upon for expertise. In addition, he or she will need to work in close partnership with the classroom teacher to create assignments, assess students' work, and establish initial collaborative relationships.

Some schools are now encouraging students to participate in network discussion groups such as KidsNet. Such participation may help to foster the development of collaborative relationships that extend beyond the boundaries of the classroom. Relatively untapped resources for collaborative learning are the multi-user environments currently available on the Internet. These textual virtual reality environments are very attractive to middle school and high school students who respond well to the simulated fantasy ambiance that characterize most current examples. The role-playing, which is an integral part of such multi-user environments, can be both instructive and liberating for students who are finding it difficult to communicate with parents, teachers, and even their peers during the difficult years of adolescence.

Although most of these multi-user environments have taken a fantasy-literature theme, one recent project may provide a model for K-12 educators wishing to put some distance between education and video games. Diversity University, a MOO that is currently being built, will provide a virtual university campus to support distance learning. Similar environments could be built to help students explore educational learning at the K-12 level.

The fostering of collaboration in the library media center, whether face-to-face or computer-mediated, will require fundamental changes in the current models of information gathering and processing, and in the physical environment of the library media center.

Short-Range Planning

Short-range strategic educational planning will be required to coordinate the adoption of the new models, to implement new curricula, and to plan for the education and training of existing library media specialists as the process unfolds. Such adaptive strategies are necessary for both educational and research purposes. The new models will not be successfully implemented, nor will their appropriateness or impact be measurable, unless the professionals responsible for the implementation are well informed and adequately trained.

Training and Education

Practicing library media specialists will need to be brought up to speed on the implications of constructivist learning theories, multiple intelligences theory, communication theory, and collaborative learning theory for the library media center environment of the future. In addition, training in the emerging technologies must be provided. Practical strategies for incorporating these theories and technologies into the library media center must be modeled through in-service workshops and training sessions. Assisted implementation may be necessary until such time that the library media specialist has successfully made the transition from print-bound to computer-mediated models of information learning.

Additional education and training will be necessary to prepare library media specialists to successfully incorporate emerging technologies into the curriculum during this interim period. For example, the library media center might provide a course in multimedia technology and design similar to the "Multimedia Structure, Organization, Access and Production" course currently taught in the MLS program at Rutgers University. This course could be taught in the place of the traditional audiovisual course in the master's curriculum. In-service training programs on the use of electronic information resources such as Learning Link, Prodigy, DIALOG

Classmate, and the Internet will be necessary for practicing library media specialists. Another interesting approach is to provide a professional development course on how to create a digital school library.

Long-Range Planning

The successful adoption of the new interaction models and incorporation of the emerging technologies will require careful long-range planning and curricula design. Too often, in the past, schools have become discouraged by the false promises of the wonders new technologies will bring to learning. Educators, however, must accept the lion's share of the burden for those failures. The emerging technologies, like their predecessors, are tools. To the extent that curricula are designed to use them well, transformation will be seen. Allowing these technologies to sit in classrooms and library media centers collecting dust is the only failure.

In addition to curricular design, ongoing education and training are crucial to the successful implementation of the emerging technologies. Long-range strategic educational planning will be required to ensure that education of library media specialists remains focused on process-oriented information learning and that timely training in technological innovation is provided. This will require cooperation among the K-12 schools involved, the master's programs that prepare future library media candidates, and professional development programs that offer courses to practicing professionals who need to update their knowledge and skills.

CONCLUSIONS

Preparing to meet the challenges that will accompany the integration of emerging technologies into the library media center is not an easy task. The successful integration of multimedia, networking, and virtual reality technologies will not only further the gradual metamorphosis from library to media center, it will transform an infrastructure that supported quiet, independent study and placed a high value on reading and text-based learning into one that encourages the appreciation of multiple intelligences and values communication and collaboration. Though this sort of transformation would appear to be within the guidelines proposed in *Information Power* (American Association of School Librarians 1988), little exists in the way of a support structure to ease the transition. Technological and monetary barriers are disappearing, but psychological and educational barriers still loom large. The emerging technologies need to be incorporated into master's and professional development programs and teacher in-service training to make this transition possible. Attention needs to be directed beyond technical education—though that is also necessary—to fundamental issues such as restructuring the library media center environment, adopting models that acknowledge the richness and diversity of the information learning process, and revaluing communication and collaboration as tools for learning. The library media specialist who successfully meets these challenges will create a vital environment central to the K-12 educational experience.

REFERENCES

American Association of School Librarians. 1988. *Information Power: Guidelines for School Library Media Programs*. Chicago: American Library Association.

Belkin, N. 1980. "Anomolous States of Knowledge for Information Retrieval." *Canadian Journal of Information Science* 5: 133-43.

Buckland, M. 1992. *Redesigning Library Services: A Manifesto*. Chicago: American Library Association.

Eisenberg, M. B., and R. E. Berkowitz. 1990. *Information Problem-Solving: The Big Six Skills Approach to Library & Information Skills Instruction*. Norwood, NJ: Ablex.

Gardner, H. 1983. *Frames of Mind: The Theory of Multiple Intelligences*. New York: Basic Books.

Hamm, M., and D. Adams. 1992. *The Collaborative Dimensions of Learning*. Norwood, NJ: Ablex.

Harel, I., and S. Papert, eds. 1991. *Constructionism: Research Reports and Essays, 1985-1990*. Norwood, NJ: Ablex.

Kuhlthau, C. 1993. *Seeking Meaning: A Process Approach to Library and Information Services*. Norwood, NJ: Ablex.

13

Distance Education for Teacher-Librarianship
Learning from Programs in Australia

ℝ **DIANNE OBERG** ⅋

Access to programs of teacher-librarianship education has been and continues to be a concern in Canada. The programs are small, few in number, and spread out over a very large geographic area.[1] In the United States also there are access concerns. Since 1988, the Library and Information Science Distance Education Consortium (LISDEC) has been working toward providing greater access to school library media education for students who are constrained by barriers such as time, distance, and personal or professional commitments.[2] Because Australia has long been a leader in distance education, including distance education for teacher-librarians, and because Australian education is not vastly different from ours, North Americans can learn much from their experiences in this field. This article describes four distance education programs in teacher-librarianship investigated by the author during a six-week study visit to southeastern Australia, identifies some common themes and approaches, and suggests some key learnings related to the provision of distance education programs.

WHAT IS DISTANCE EDUCATION?

Much of the current literature about distance education focuses on the use of computer and video technology for distance education delivery. However, distance education does not depend on sophisticated delivery systems. A decade ago, over 90 percent of distance education programs were delivered by means of print materials supplemented by audiovisual materials.[3] There appear not to have been major changes in this pattern, primarily because of the immense cost of such technologies as interactive multimedia[4] and also because of concerns related to instructional effectiveness and student access.[5] High-cost technologies have not proven to be more effective than low-cost, simple technologies such as correspondence and audioconferencing.[6] The fiber optic systems now connecting some urban centers in North America are not accessible by many of the very students who want and need access to distance education programs.

139

Distance education is best defined not by any particular medium but by four general elements or conditions: 1) the separation of teacher and learner during at least the majority of the instructional process; 2) the influence of an educational organization, including the provision of student evaluation; 3) the use of educational media to unite teacher and learner and carry course content; and 4) the provision of two-way communication between the learner and teacher, tutor, or educational agency.[7] Distance education involves both teaching at a distance and learning at a distance.

The concept of *distance* as separation of teacher and student is basic to a theoretical framework for distance education. That separation can be understood in terms of structure and dialogue.[8] Structure involves the extent to which a program can be shaped by student needs. A high-structure program is typified by precisely defined objectives, by detailed study guides, and by common assignments, deadlines, and examinations. A high-structure program is generally less responsive to the interests and needs of individual students. Dialogue involves the provision of two-way communication between teacher and student. A high-dialogue program provides many opportunities for interaction between teacher and student. There is no one preferred level of structure and dialogue for all programs. Each program should be developed with the structure and dialogue that is most appropriate to its intended participants.

Garrison points out that distance education and conventional or face-to-face education are more alike than they are different.[9] What is essential to all education is the communication between (and among) teachers and students, a two-way communication that enables the learners (both teachers and students) to transform information into knowledge. Effective education, whether in a distance mode or in a face-to-face mode, must involve persistent and ongoing dialogue and discussion that enlarges and deepens the understandings of both teachers and students. Distance education differs from face-to-face education primarily in terms of the organization of the components of the educational transaction. How the components of that educational transaction are organized is critical to the success of the distance education programs described in this article.

DIPLOMA PROGRAMS IN
TEACHER-LIBRARIANSHIP EDUCATION

As in Canada and the United States, there are many routes available in Australia for teacher-librarianship education. Some universities in Australia provide this education as part of a four-year teacher education program. Some provide it through a one-year diploma after teaching certification and experience. A few provide it through a two-year master's degree, often a research-based degree. Programs in teacher-librarianship education are accredited through ALIA, the Australian Library and Information Association.

This article focuses on those programs of teacher-librarianship education requiring one year of study beyond teacher certification. In Canada, the equivalent programs would be called Diploma or Graduate Diploma programs (24-30 credit hours). The equivalent programs in the United States would be those providing initial certification for school library media specialists, usually non-ALA-accredited library education programs, involving 21-30 credit hours of study.[10] These one-year programs provide basic training for entry into practice as a teacher-librarian or a library media specialist.

To enter the diploma programs for teacher-librarianship in Australia, students must have a teaching certificate and teaching experience. Teacher certification generally requires three or four years of university-level education and one year of successful teaching experience. Many Australian teachers begin their careers with a three-year teaching qualification and then, after some classroom experience, complete an additional year of training to attain a bachelor of education or an equivalent four-year qualification.

The author was in contact with four universities offering diploma programs in teacher-librarianship by distance education. Each of the four universities offers other library education programs that are not addressed in this report. Clearly, this report should not be assumed to be a comprehensive picture of education for teacher-librarians in Australia. It is limited geographically to the southeastern part of Australia. It is limited by a focus on programs of a certain type (one-year diploma programs) offered in a certain way (by distance education). To give some sense of the programs, each of the descriptions below will address the number of courses in the program, both required and elective; the approximate time for program completion; the number of students enrolled; and the number of faculty involved, in absolute numbers and in full-time equivalents (FTE).

PROGRAM DESCRIPTIONS

University of South Australia, Magill Campus
Adelaide, South Australia

The Graduate Diploma in Teacher-Librarianship requires the completion of the following six courses that can be completed over a three-year period: Literature for School Libraries, Resource Development, School Library Management, Information Retrieval, Bibliographic Control, and Librarian as Teacher. Some study school attendance is required. There are approximately 70 students in the distance mode Graduate Diploma program. There are four faculty members teaching in the Graduate Diploma program (2 FTE). Each instructor is responsible for one course per semester.

Monash University, Gippsland Campus
Churchill, Victoria

The Graduate Diploma of Education (School Librarianship) requires the completion of eight courses and a practicum. Students normally complete the program over a two-year period. The courses are: Language, Literacy, and Literature in Education; Foundations of School Librarianship; Administration and Organization of the Resource Center; Curriculum Planning and Resources; Information Needs and Users; Organization of Information; Computer Supported Information Services; and Special Topics in School Librarianship. The School Librarianship Practicum involves 20 days of supervised practical experience in a library staffed by a trained, experienced librarian; the School Librarianship Professional Development involves undertaking 10 different professional activities such as library visits and participation in in-service sessions and conferences. Attendance at study schools is strongly recommended. There are approximately 65 students in the distance mode Graduate Diploma program. Four faculty members (4 FTE) are involved full time in teaching the program. Each instructor is responsible for one course per semester.

Charles Sturt University, Riverina Campus
Wagga Wagga, New South Wales

The Graduate Diploma in Education (Teacher-Librarianship) requires the completion of eight courses and a practicum. About half the students complete the program in two years; the others take a third year to complete requirements. The courses are: Teacher Librarianship, Children's Literature, Information Dissemination, Technology, Collection Development, Organization of Resources, Management, and Topics. The practicum, called Professional Practice, involves a two-week placement at a special or public library, a four-day group-study visit to libraries or to a conference, and three other individual professional activities. There are optional study schools for seven of the courses. There are approximately 200 students in the distance mode Graduate Diploma program. Four faculty members (4 FTE) are involved in teaching the program. Each instructor is responsible for two courses per semester.

Queensland University of Technology, Kelvin Grove Campus
Brisbane, Queensland

The Graduate Diploma in Education (Teacher-Librarianship) requires the completion of six core courses and two elective courses. The core courses are: Foundations of Teacher-Librarianship, Curriculum and Related Resources, Literature and Literacy: Resources and Strategies, School Library Resources: Organization and Access, Communication and Management in School Library Resource Centers, and Information Services for Schools. The elective courses are: Australian Literature for Young People, Books and Publishing, Interactive Technologies in Education, Literacy Education and Libraries, Literature for Young People, Media Literacy and the School, Reference Services and Materials, Resource Services for Special Needs, Storytelling, and Visual Literacy and Resource Design. Special seminar courses are organized in response to special needs and/or the availability of special expertise; directed-study courses are organized for individuals with special interests beyond core and elective course offerings. The practicum component of this program is incorporated into core courses and involves school experience, 25 hours of work with a teacher-librarian, and field activities, 35 hours of professional activities. Until 1993, all students took the first half of the program on campus full-time and the second half part-time, by distance study or by evening classes on campus. Now students may take the program in a variety of ways, including a fully distance study mode. Today, approximately 20 of the total 150 students in the program are on-campus full-time students. Five faculty members (4.5 FTE) are involved in teaching the program. Each instructor is responsible for two or three courses per semester.

THE NATURE OF THE PROGRAMS

The programs described above operate within what is called, in the distance education literature, an integrated or mixed mode model. In this model, the one used by most distance education providers at the university level in Australia, one or several departments within a university offer programs to both internal and external students. Usually the same academic staff are responsible for working with both on-campus and distance education students.

Courses are generally scheduled over a four-month academic term, whether the course is being delivered to internal or external students. The academic year at Australian universities is divided into two semesters, one beginning in February, the other in July. Distance education courses for the diploma programs are delivered by mail packages, which basically are printed course manuals and readings, and supplemented by audiotapes and videotapes, where appropriate. Some programs involve audioconferencing activities; none at this time are using videoconferencing as a regular mode of course delivery.

All offer study schools, on-campus sessions one to five days in length, organized for face-to-face teaching and learning. Study schools are sometimes called residential schools (because the students live on or near campus) or vacation schools (because they are scheduled during school holiday periods). Study schools may be a required part of a program, but increasingly they are optional. Some faculty commented that the study schools might be regarded as somewhat of a contradiction in a distance study program, and others questioned the practice of mandatory study schools in terms of unequal or restricted access for the very students that most need distance education.

Programs of distance education for teacher-librarianship have a relatively long history in Australia, some dating back to the 1970s. The four programs described above are successful ones according to a number of criteria. All are accredited by ALIA and generally attract more applicants that can be accommodated. They are academically demanding programs that also have high completion rates (over 80 percent).

Two themes emerged from the discussions with faculty members that may help to explain the high program completion rate for these programs. One coordinator reported that the completion rates for that particular program had steadily grown from 35 percent at the beginning of the program to 65 percent in the mid-1980s to a current high of 85 percent. Although the coordinator attributed this to an educational climate that both encourages teachers to upgrade their education to the equivalent of a four-year degree and ties teacher promotion to continuing education, he also conceded that the faculty worked hard to develop high-quality course materials and maintain contact with students. Every faculty member interviewed emphasized the critical importance of two aspects of their programs: instructional design and student contact.

These distance education diploma programs can be characterized as high-structure and high-dialogue programs. In most of these programs there are few options, and students are expected to follow a recommended course sequence. Course materials are quite detailed and feature clearly defined learning objectives, extensive readings, and common assignments and deadlines. Careful thought and attention are given to the design of the mail packages. All the programs are using the services of instructional designers to some degree. A great emphasis is placed on careful writing and on precise and clear directions. There is a significant commitment of time to the process. The minimum time suggested by instructors for the writing of materials for a course was the amount of time equivalent to that required for teaching a course—that is, the time required for preparing, delivering, and grading a course in the face-to-face mode. The time required would increase substantially if audiovisual materials or computer-based programs had to be developed for a course. Instructors stated that they believed that students benefited from this careful attention to high-quality course materials. In their opinion, more thought and care had to be put into materials for external students than is sometimes put into those for face-to-face students. They also suggested that the accountability factor is heightened for their programs because distance education course materials are subject to more public scrutiny than materials produced for face-to-face teaching.

Careful thought and attention were also given to dialogue—that is, to developing and maintaining close personal contact with the students. This was achieved in various ways in the different programs. Instructors were very aware of the importance of two-way communication, particularly at the start of a program, for enhancing student motivation and commitment. Often the program information booklets included pictures of the instructors as well as information about their personal interests and their academic and professional qualifications. Students were asked to reciprocate with pictures and with information about their personal and professional commitments as well as their academic backgrounds and work experience. Study schools, at the beginning of the program and with subsequent courses, offered the opportunity for students and teachers to get to know each other and to develop some sense of the institution offering their program. Students were encouraged to telephone or fax their instructors. Students were given assistance if they wished to be in contact with other students taking the program in their geographic area. Audioconferencing was used for class discussions, and some programs were using electronic mail systems for communication between and among teachers and students. In one program, faculty organized group-study visits to libraries in various centers for their students; these study visits offered students the chance to meet faculty and other students in addition to the chance to learn about their profession and their professional community. At conferences and other professional meetings, faculty often arranged to meet with students. These opportunities were believed to be particularly important for students living in very remote areas.

In summary, it appears that much of the success of the four programs can be attributed to the support that they provide for student learning, both through course design and student contact. These distance education programs for teacher-librarianship were investigated in order to assess the possibilities of developing a Canadian program. The learnings with which this article concludes are those that were key for the author, perhaps those she most needed to learn. Other investigators with other interests or concerns might have identified quite different learnings.

KEY LEARNINGS

Teaching and learning at a distance need not involve complex technology. What is more important is using our knowledge of how students learn. This was emphasized even by those instructors working in units with access to multimedia publishing and computer conferencing systems. Print materials were first developed with thoughtful consideration to the cognitive and affective characteristics and needs of the students. Even where units were pressing their own multimedia CD masters, the instructors emphasized that print materials remained the backbone and the starting point for course design. Two-way videoconferencing systems were not seen as a panacea. Instead, some instructors cautioned that they might represent a step backward because they could easily be used to replicate at a distance the worst abuses of face-to-face lecturing. Tutorials, on the other hand, were seen as an instructional strategy that could be facilitated by this technology, although the advantages of this over the much less expensive audioconferencing are not yet proven.

Distance education programs can make effective use of technology to increase the efficiency of course development and student support systems. Electronic document production systems simplify the process of developing and producing course materials and allow efficiencies in inventory and in revision of materials, whatever the medium chosen for course materials. Computerized systems reduce the time devoted to the record keeping necessary for registration and program planning and for tracking student assessment and course completion. Instructor time and office staff time is saved when barcode-reading equipment can be used for tracking the mailing of students' materials and the receipt and return of their assignments. At one of the universities, student messages and questions are recorded in a database so that they can be easily analyzed for use in improving the university's responsiveness to student needs and concerns. The use of technology in these and other ways increases the time available for course development and for contact with students.

Distance education programs for teacher-librarianship can be designed to provide the essential professional-learning experiences that are part of conventional face-to-face programs. Instructors in each of the programs had devised ways for students to experience a practicum and to engage in professional-development activities. The programs were also planned to meet the unique characteristics of the students. Because the students involved in education for teacher-librarianship are generally experienced teachers and learners, they are able to handle a considerable amount of choice within courses, especially in course assignments. Choices were provided within a structured program, however, because the students are entering a new field with specific competencies to be attained. Maintaining some of the structures of a face-to-face class, such as common starting and ending dates, recommended timelines for coursework, and assignment deadlines, appears to help busy students, most of them working, many full time, to complete the program.

Garrison argues that distance education programs need to emphasize independence less and interdependence more.[11] The distance education programs for teacher-librarianship described here appear to have found a way to strike a dynamic balance between independence and interdependence, where the control of teaching and learning is shared in a way that meets students' learning needs. Students are learn independently and when they are supported in their learning by well-designed courses and by interaction with their instructor and with the other students in the courses.

NOTES

1. Larry Amey, *Education for Teacher Librarians in Canada: A National Study* (Ottawa, Ontario: Canadian School Library Association, 1992).

2. Daniel D. Barron, "Distance Education and School Library Media Specialists," in *School Library Media Annual, 1991*, edited by Jane Bandy Smith and J. Gordon Coleman, Jr. (Englewood, CO: Libraries Unlimited, 1990), 20-29.

3. Chris Curran, "Factors Affecting Costs of Media in Distance Education, " in *Media and Technology in European Distance Education*, edited by A. W. Bates (Heerlen, The Netherlands: European Association of Distance Teaching Universities, 1989), 27-39.

4. Ibid.

5. Marvin Van Kekerix and James Andrews, "Electronic Media and Independent Study," in *The Foundations of American Distance Education*, edited by Barbara L. Watkins and Stephen J. Wright (Dubuque, IA: Kendall/Hunt, 1991), 135-57.

6. Thomas L. Russell, "Television's Indelible Impact on Distance Education: What We Should Have Learned from Comparative Research," *Research in Distance Education* 4 (October 1992): 2-4.

7. John R. Verduin, Jr. and Thomas A. Clark, *Distance Education: The Foundations of Effective Practice* (San Francisco: Jossey-Bass, 1991), 11.

8. Desmond Keegan, *Foundations of Distance Education*, 2d ed. (London: Routledge, 1990).

9. D. G. Garrison, *Understanding Distance Education: A Framework for the Future* (London: Routledge, 1989).

10. Selvin W. Royal, "Profile of Selected Characteristics of Non-ALA Accredited Library Education Programs: Part 2, Curriculum," in *School Library Media Annual, 1991*, edited by Jane Bandy Smith and J. Gordon Coleman (Englewood, CO: Libraries Unlimited, 1990), 165-81.

11. Garrison, *Understanding Distance Education*.

The author acknowledges with thanks the hospitality and the generosity of a number of instructors and other faculty members in Australia, in particular: Maureen Nimon, University of South Australia, Magill; Joe Hallein and Judy Phillips, Monash University, Gippsland; James Henri, Sue Britton, Ken Dillon, and Ashley Freeman, Charles Sturt University, Riverina; Ross Todd and Barbara Poston-Anderson, University of Technology Sydney, Kuring-gai; Paul Lupton and Geoff Chapman, Queensland University of Technology, Kelvin Grove; Ivan Williams and John Barrett, University of Southern Queensland, Toowoomba. Their assistance was invaluable and their patience admirable. Any errors of fact or interpretation are entirely the author's.

14

Uses of Telecommunication
in K-12 Education
An Institute in Print

ℜ **KATHLEEN GARLAND** ℘

Telecommunication has great potential to provide information for students and teachers, information beyond that available in their library media centers and textbooks. Telecommunication is what makes possible the "library without walls," also known as the virtual library or the digital library.

IMPORTANCE OF THE
VIRTUAL LIBRARY CONCEPT

Whatever it may be called, the virtual library concept is being discussed in a variety of public forums. *Newsweek* and *Time* magazines have devoted cover stories and feature articles to the virtual library. The lead-off article in the October 1993 issue of the Association for Supervision and Curriculum Development's newsletter, *Update*, highlighted the virtual library.[1] Network television has covered the virtual library. Professional journals are awash with references to the information super-highway, the Internet, as an information conduit.

The Internet, the network of networks, encircles the globe. Users can search databases located continents away and converse via electronic mail with other users who may be sitting at their computers halfway around the world or at the end of the block. The first users of this network were research scientists working for the government, and even today researchers and other academics form the core of users of this vast network.

The U.S. government is interested, however, in expanding the base of network users to include the general public and the schools. The government, through the National Science Foundation, will be distributing millions of dollars over the next several years to universities, industry, and education for further exploration and development of model programs. Within the current Administration, Dr. Milton Halem, Chief of NASA's Space Data and Computing Division, was keynote speaker at a recent workshop, "The Role of K-12 Education in Digital Libraries." He considers the digital library to be a "collaboratory" in which users communicate,

147

create, add to, and revise the library's holdings. Halem spoke of NASA's efforts to fund test sites in Washington, D.C. and suburban Maryland secondary schools, where students and teachers are exploring ways to use the vast amount of information available via the Internet. NASA has data that it would like to make easily accessible, and is funding studies to explore ways to foster accessibility.

The legislative branch of government is also convinced of the importance of this new technology for K-12 schools. In 1993, the Technology for Education Act (S.1040) was introduced in the Senate. It would provide funding for Internet connections and for training for school personnel in the use of technology.

IMPORTANCE OF TRAINING

Training is the key. Library media specialists and teachers must know how to use technology and how it might be applicable in their classrooms. If these conditions are not met, the history of technology in education might repeat itself. Just because a technology exists and is available in schools does not mean that it will be widely used. Larry Cuban's book on the history of educational technology amply documents this point.[2]

The Department of Education, through the Office of Library Programs, recognizes the importance of staff training and is funding institutes for school library media specialists. In August of 1994, the School of Information and Library Studies (SILS) at the University of Michigan presented one of these institutes, "Uses of Telecommunication in K-12 Education." Attendance at institutes such as this one is necessarily limited by the amount of equipment on site and the number of staff available to provide individual attention to participants.

DESIGN OF THE INSTITUTE

The purpose of this institute is to introduce building-level school library media specialists to the variety of information resources that may be accessed on the Internet and to provide them with experience in merging textual information from the Internet with visuals to create an educational product. In effect, participants use the virtual library available through the Internet and adding value to it. This institute empowers participants to be building-level technology specialists in telecommunications, specialists who teach other library media specialists, teachers, and students. To multiply the effects of the institute's training, attendees are required to present at least one telecommunication workshop upon return home.

The rationale for the design of this institute is based on research that has identified factors associated with successful implementation of change and successful workshop structure. The configuration of instruction for the institute is as follows: lecture and readings, demonstration, hands-on activities (guided practice and feedback), and coaching. The coaching aspect is particularly innovative. Participants will be given an account on the SILS server to enable them to interact with each other and gain support from designated institute staff for four months afterward. In other words, by making use of what they have learned, participants will be receiving the encouragement and support they need to successfully implement changes at their various localities.

OVERVIEW OF INSTITUTE ACTIVITIES

We have endeavored to keep this institute simple in the following ways: 1) with relatively low-cost and easy-to-use equipment like visualizers, scanners, and computers with which participants are already familiar; 2) with inexpensive software that is easy to use; and 3) with narrowly focused end-products created by small groups that have similar interests.

This institute is the product of many people who are pooling their expertise, and as such it may be replicated by others using local talent from their areas. Although the institute as planned and as presented here spans five consecutive days, it can easily be reconfigured.

DAY 1

Morning
Introduction and Welcome

Keynote: "Networking Our Nation's Schools"

Telecommunications overview
(basic information on telecommunications terminology, how it functions, and how it is developing)

Local and wide area networks overview
(introduction to terminology and technology)

Afternoon
Introduction to electronic networks:
Bulletin boards
General commercial electronic networks (e.g., America Online)
K-12 commercial networks (e.g., National Geographic Kids Network)

Introducing the Internet
(overview of Gopher, WAIS, etc. and types of resources available on the Internet)

K-12 sources of information on the Internet
(overview of resources of interest to students and teachers in the K-12 environment)

Evening
Grouping into teams to begin projects
(begins process of identifying practical, attendee-selected projects to be worked on by 5-6 people over the next four days; projects provide basis for the hands-on skill-building activities that follow)

Hands-on Internet exploration
(hands-on experience in a guided Internet exercise)

Day 2

Morning

Feedback from Day 1
(based on one-minute paper evaluations of previous day's activities, this feedback will guide staff in making any adjustments necessary to fit individual participant's needs and provide participants with a useful source of help in their own future-workshop planning)

Focused Internet exploration to find project-related information

Afternoon

Introduction to using Internet resources on a local database
(demonstration on combining text from the Internet with other media formats)

Planning for local networks and file-servers

Local networks and file-servers: Issues of rights and permissions

Networks and file-servers implemented: Examples from schools

Evening

Focused Internet exploration *or*

Capture tools—visualizer, base scanner, Xapshot, etc.

Day 3

Morning

Feedback from Day 2

Team project planning, implementation, product design
(attendees begin the task of carrying out specific projects, and learning and practicing media conversion skills)

Technology for populating a local network: Capturing digital input
(demonstration and hands-on experience digitizing video and text)

Afternoon

Imaging systems and related technologies—scanning, etc.
(demonstration and hands-on experience with user-friendly equipment)

Evening

Teams work on selected projects in supervised labs

Day 4

Morning

Feedback from Day 3

Teams work on projects in labs

Afternoon
Teams work on projects in labs

Evening
Teams work on projects in labs

Day 5

Morning
Feedback from Day 4

Viewing and critiquing of team projects by staff and participants

Imaging vendors provide information on hardware and software

Budgeting: Networked resources and services

Afternoon
Keeping connected, introduction to:
Electronic bulletin board for Institute participants
Electronic mail system
Assignment of passwords and practice using e-mail

Strategies and processes for successfully developing and implementing workshops upon return home

Review of overheads and other Institute materials useful to participants for presenting their own workshops

Wrap-Up: Envisioning the Digital Library
(a full-circle look back at the keynote address and consideration of the school library media specialist's role in creating, accessing, and using the emerging electronic resources networks)

Post-Institute Activities

Electronic access to Institute staff is provided for four months.

Electronic access to Institute bulletin board is provided.

NOTES

1. John O'Neil, "Using Technology to Support 'Authentic' Learning," *Update* 35 (October 1993):1+.

2. Larry Cuban, *Teachers and Machines: The Classroom Use of Technology Since 1920* (New York: Teachers College Press, 1986).

Index

153